"Radical Obedience: The Chronicles of Two Global Pilgrims":
I have known Paul Alexander since the night he began the journey described in this book. Little did I realize what I was being privileged to witness, what quiet power was entering the Kingdom, what trouble the smile on that young face signaled for the powers of darkness! When he and Carol joined up, that trouble was multiplied! This is a wonderful, fast-moving account of their "life together", that grips and draws you into re-living what is their God-ordained, Christ-centered and Spirit-empowered journey of discipleship. It includes an invitation at each juncture to join them! It makes the call to such discipleship normative and reveals it as a fun-filled adventure of growth and change, risk and reward. It celebrates the God who is there, who loves and leads, and who knows that a story lived in Him, always ends well. Read this book - it will inspire and empower you!

Costa Mitchell
Former National Director
Vineyard Churches South Africa

What a delightful read! This book will inspire you with honest down-to-earth stories of God's extraordinary faithfulness, in response to the faith and obedience of two humble servants of Jesus. Paul and Carol Alexander's courageous "trust and obey" attitude, in the words of the hymn, is a model for all followers of Jesus. Their stories show how God's unfolding plan and purpose led to many miracles, not without testing and sacrifice. This half century real life adventure in God's Kingdom, will draw you to deeper levels of surrender to God's call on your life. Paul and Carol's story reminds me of Nietzsche's words, "The essential thing in heaven and earth is that there should be a long obedience in the same direction; there thereby results, and has always resulted in the long run, something which has made life worth living".

Alexander F Venter
Vineyard pastor, theologian, author.

'Radical Obedience' is a book that is written for the generations coming through who would bravely choose to step out in faith. Young people need to hear the stories of faith of those who have gone before to remind them to step forward regardless of any obstacles and fulfil the call of God on their lives. Paul and Carol have modelled to me personally as well as thousands of young people what it is to live the great adventure of serving Jesus and we are grateful for their example. My prayer is that this book would inspire many to take great leaps of faith, obeying God to see a world impacted with the gospel.

Hannah Williamson
Young Lions Lead & Church Planter (Young Lions is a young leaders program for 15-19 year olds based out of AoG GB)

Many Christians instinctively know that God calls them to a life of obedience, and yet many things stand in the way of doing exactly that. Well, this book is like a compass that reorients a person to that which leads to a meaningful Christian life. I don't say 'successful Christian life' because obedience to God, let alone Radical Obedience, might not lead to success in the eyes of many. Thankfully, Drs. Paul and Carol Alexander picked up early on that life is about the audience of one, and that is God. As they both narrate, everything for them began in my home country of South Africa, when each, separately, surrendered their lives to Jesus in their early teens. Following that, they picked up a key that they are graciously sharing here. Read and unlock your world.

Afrika Mhlope, Author, TV producer and International Speaker.

"Radial Obedience: The Chronicles of Two Global Pilgrims" is a first-hand testimony to the power of saying yes to God's call, no matter the cost. Paul and Carol Alexander, tracing the fruit of obedience, share a deeply personal journey of faith and sacrifice. Their story of obedience spans continents and decades, revealing how influence is multiplied through unwavering devotion to the Lord and each other. This book is an inspiring reminder that genuine global impact flows from lives fully surrendered.

Dr. Michael J. Beals President, Vanguard University

Dr. Paul and Dr. Carol Alexander have lived a life marked by unwavering faith and radical obedience to God's call. In Radical Obedience: The Chronicles of Two Global Pilgrims, they share their remarkable journey—from the blossoming of young love to the adventures of life's greatest challenges.

This book is more than a memoir; it is a call to every believer to reflect on their own obedience to God. Through their compelling narrative, the Alexanders remind us that true fulfillment is found in surrendering to God's will, even when the path is uncertain. Their story will inspire, challenge, and ignite a renewed passion to walk in obedience, no matter the cost.

I highly recommend this book to anyone longing to deepen their faith through radical obedience to God's call.

Dr. Darryl Wootton
Superintendent of Oklahoma Assemblies of God

Radical Obedience unveils the incredible, life-altering power of the Gospel, showing how the lives of two individuals were set on an entirely new trajectory —one that sparked a ripple effect, changing countless lives around the world.

Gene Roncone, Leader, Rocky Mountain AG Ministry Network.

"Radical Obedience: The Chronicles of Two Global Pilgrims" is a powerful and deeply personal account of what it means to live a life fully surrendered to God's call. Having known Paul and Carol for over 30 years, first as pastors in inner city Brisbane, Australia, and later as Bible College Leads in the UK, I have witnessed firsthand their unwavering faith, sacrificial obedience, and unrelenting commitment to the Gospel. This book is more than a memoir; it is an invitation to step into a life of radical trust in God, no matter the cost. Their journey will inspire, challenge, and stir your heart toward a deeper walk with Christ. A must-read for anyone longing to live with courage, faith, and purpose!"

Ps Glyn Barrett
Senior Pastor !Audacious Church
National Leader Assemblies of God Great Britain

Adventure in God's kingdom doesn't always look like what we expect— it can be thrilling, unpredictable, and at times, even disappointing. In Radical Obedience: The Chronicles of Two Global Pilgrims, Drs. Paul and Carol share how a life surrendered to Jesus leads to a journey they never could have imagined. Guided by prophetic words, divine encounters, and unwavering faith, their story beautifully portrays God's grace on those who discern and follow His voice. Dr. Paul writes in the book, "Loving Jesus and serving His people would define the rest of our lives". Their journey is a powerful testament to that calling. This book will certainly inspire those on the adventure of bold faith and radical obedience in Jesus.

Aaron Phoenix
North Dakota Assemblies of God Student Ministries Director

The Alexanders are incredible! God has used their lives to transform the lives of others across the globe. God speaks through them! As such, I would strongly recommend this book to every person seeking to transform their lives and the lives of others in the most profound and godly manner.

Dr. Sandra Ogunremi,
Healthcare Executive and South Dakota Assemblies of God Women's Director

How Christians live is the best proof of what they believe. Paul and Carol Alexander have demonstrated a willingness to follow Jesus Christ wherever He leads - in their case, across five decades, four continents, and various ministry assignments as pastors, missionaries, and educators. Their memoir is a testimony of radical obedience, as well as an inspiration for us to follow. This book is certain to bless you and mentor you toward excellence in discipleship.

Donna Barrett, General Secretary, Assemblies of God (USA)

Radical Obedience

THE CHRONICLES OF TWO GLOBAL PILGRIMS

PAUL AND CAROL ALEXANDER

WESTBOW
PRESS®
A DIVISION OF THOMAS NELSON
& ZONDERVAN

WestBow Press books may be ordered through booksellers or by contacting:

WestBow Press
A Division of Thomas Nelson & Zondervan
1663 Liberty Drive
Bloomington, IN 47403
www.westbowpress.com
844-714-3454

ISBN: 979-8-3850-4807-6 (sc)
ISBN: 979-8-3850-4806-9 (e)

Library of Congress Control Number: 2025907430

Print information available on the last page.

WestBow Press rev. date: 5/12/2025

Dedication

For our students past and present
In the hope that they will see a vibrant Bible
College movement in their generation
And for Ava and Ty
That your lives would be wholly committed to
Jesus and His cause. We love you!

Contents

Foreword

In today's cultural context, obedience (let alone radical obedience) is a word that can carry with it a weight of hesitation and reluctance. It implies submission, yielding, and surrender—biblical ideals that stand in stark contrast to ideals of independence, self-reliance, and personal ambition. Yet, in the pages of this book, two willing servants of God reveal a different kind of obedience—one that is neither passive nor forced but rather radical, life-giving, and transformative.

My wife Amy and I have had the honor of getting to know Paul and Carol Alexander as dear friends for the last several years. Every time we have spent time with them, we walk away blessed and encouraged in so many ways. Truthfully, we often wish we knew them well before we were first introduced! While we cannot go back in time and relive life experiences with them, this book provides profound insights from two servants of God who chose radical obedience in pursuit of God's plan for their lives.

Radical Obedience: The Chronicles of Two Global Pilgrims is more than a memoir; it is a testament to the faithfulness of God and the willingness of two ordinary people to say "yes" to His extraordinary call. Paul and Carol's story is one of unwavering faith, courage in uncertainty, and the profound joy found in surrendering to God's divine purposes. From the sunlit shores of South Africa to the bustling cities and quiet corners of the world, their journey exemplifies what it means to follow Christ without abandon.

As you read this book, you will witness how small acts of obedience lead to great impact. You will see how faithfulness in the unseen moments prepares the way for miracles. Their stories—sometimes humorous, often challenging, always inspiring—are a reminder that a life yielded to God is never wasted, but rather, is shaped into a masterpiece of divine design. Each chapter ends with an opportunity for you to reflect on facets of your own journey.

For those who are wondering if the call of God is worth the cost, this book offers an undeniable answer: YES! Though the path may be uncertain and the road steep at times, a life of radical obedience is the most fulfilling journey you can embark upon. Paul and Carol's testimony is proof that when we choose to trust and obey, we step into a life far greater than anything we could ever plan for ourselves.

May this book encourage you, challenge you, and, above all, invite you to walk boldly in your own journey of radical obedience.

Philip E. Dearborn, Ed.D.
President, Association for Biblical Higher Education

Preface

The world is a book, and those who
don't travel only read one page
AUGUSTINE OF HIPPO

CAROL

This book was being written while my precious dad was in the final phase of his life. Dad kept asking me when we were going to write our next book. I often evaded answering his question by talking to him about our busy schedule. Paul, and I knew there was another book inside our hearts but it was still percolating in our thinking. Slowly, as with any good cup of coffee, our ideas have filtered through our minds and spilled onto these pages and produced what we hope is an inspiring book.

As you will note from the title of our book, the theme is *radical obedience*. Let me assure you that obedience does not come naturally or easily to us. Our human tendency is to kick against the prompts and prods of the Divine, to scream, shout, resist, resent, refuse, until we learn that yielding our self-will and surrendering to God, is not only the best option but the safest.

The Gospels are a call to *radical obedience* for anyone who claims to be a Christ follower. Jesus called us to take up our cross and follow Him. He never promised that serving Him would be a safe and secure path; He promised that He would walk with us through every season. The apostle Paul exemplifies *radical obedience* and calls each follower of Jesus to that lifestyle. We are two ordinary people who serve an extraordinary God and share with you the reader, our attempt to walk this pathway of obedience.

Our lives have been rich and colorful, and at the same time, stretching and challenging. There have been days of almost unbearable pain and sorrow, and moments of rapturous joy. Sometimes those extreme emotions occupy the same space and it is only God's grace that sees us through. But it is those times that have made us who we are. They have strengthened our resolve to be obedient and to seek to do our Master's bidding.

Paul and I became committed Christ followers when we were both in our teens. We were both at different church camps, in the same year and month, and what occurred at those camps began a work in our lives that would eventually lead us to this moment in time. That was our beginning on the road to *radical obedience.* God's timing is always perfect because, on one side of the South African coast a 14-year-old, blonde haired, blue-eyed boy, was responding to a sense of the call of God, while at the same time, a few miles further up the same coast, a 13-year-old blonde girl, with green eyes, was also saying 'yes' to Jesus; neither realized the adventures that awaited them and that they were destined to the same calling. It amazes me to know that God was planning our lives so carefully and ensuring that our paths would cross at the perfect moment in time. That we would both encounter Jesus in the same year, in the same month, on the same coast, and hear His call has made me aware of how God is involved in the most intricate details of our lives.

So, beautiful memories, happily concealed beneath the passage of time, now surface to remind us of our journey and God's goodness, faithfulness, and enduring kindness. It is these chronicles of our lives that we now share with you.

As the sun rises with triumphant brightness and bathes my room with delightful warmth I sit to revel in those sweet memories. I find comfort in those reminiscences. As I write, I am listening to the rhythmic and soothing ticking of our old clock that has always found a secure resting place in one of the many homes in which we have lived. The delectable warmth of our library of books, many old and worn, but which have travelled with us to four continents, and 13 different houses, fills me with a sense of security and roots. Familiarity brings comfort. With the many countries and homes, in which we have lived, familiarity and security have been short lived. But then, I do remember many years ago praying a fervent prayer: 'God help me to hold loosely to the things of this world so that they never captivate me and distract me from your perfect will for my life.' It has not always been an easy path. But it has always been the best, the safest, and without hesitation, the most fulfilling.

I have had to leave my precious parents behind and as they have aged, it has been difficult living at a distance. Many times, my pillow has been wet with tears as I have watched old age creep up on them, and gradually steal mom's beautiful mind, and dad's incredible strength.

Leaving our children and grandchildren has been another one of those challenges, but Anna and Jay have helped us to walk this path of obedience by assisting us in navigating these seasons with grace. They have been unselfish and generous in their release of us, and we know they are as much a part of all we do as we are. Anna, has always ensured, when those occasions arise, that we get quality time with our two precious grandchildren. She is the most generous, godly, and caring daughter we could have hoped for. We are grateful for our supportive children and family who make serving Jesus a joy, and who have willingly carried the burden of our ministry; they have prayed earnestly, and supported us faithfully through every season and each decision we have made. We are grateful. These matters have been some of those which have to be considered when anticipating the cost of obedience. Ours has not been a life without challenges.

Mom and Dad have loved following the trajectory of all we do and have joyfully yielded their children to the service of the King. Dad was ready for his eternal abode and I do know that heaven will have got a little louder upon his entry. At ninety-seven years of age he had a good innings. I dwell on the thought of the welcome he received when he entered eternity.

How can it be that obedience is at the same time costly and beautiful? Costly because we said 'yes' to something we did not choose, beautiful, because when we obey, it becomes the only thing we ever want to do, the only place we really want to be, and the only life we truly want to live. To yield our will to the Divine is complex and simple, costly and beautiful, mystical and real. How paradoxical.

Paul and I have loved the lives we have lived and we are delighted to share these chronicles with you. We have written this book jointly because it is our story and our journey together that has birthed this narrative. So, you will see each chapter is written by one of us, and we identify whose voice you are listening to by placing our name at the beginning of the chapter.

This book is a memoir of our lives so it follows a chronological pattern. Our prayer is that our experiences will enrich and encourage your hearts and lives. For those who have never yielded to Jesus, our desire is that every page you turn will entice you to continue reading and so glimpse the magnificent Jesus that we have served. We love Him with every fiber of our beings and we want every day of our lives to be impactful for His kingdom.

I started this preface talking about my dad, and the fact that he was at the entrance of the gate of heaven. We have this innate tendency to avoid the topic of death because who wants to talk about dying when we are trying to get through each day? Henri Nouwen, said that dying is not something we should fear because dying is only the beginning for believers in Christ. He went on to say that we all have choices and we make them every day of our lives. We choose to make each day count or we cling to anger, bitterness and unforgiveness. We can cleave tenaciously to life and die with bitterness and anger or we can choose to let go when the time comes and leave with the hope of the resurrection that infuses us and those we leave behind. We choose the way we live and those choices ultimately impact the way we die. We can make our death a gift to those we leave behind or we leave them with unhappy memories.

Death should not be morbid but it should be sobering. The Bible reminds us that life is like a vapor that appears for a short time and then vanishes. The purpose of this book is a call to obedience and service. It is also an appeal for a proper and right response to God's call for His kingdom 'to come on earth as it is in heaven.' I hope and pray that we will all choose wisely how we will live, and eventually, if our lives are not suddenly snatched away by some unfortunate accident, we can choose to die well.

We deliberately end each chapter with a section entitled, 'prayerful pause.' This allows for a time to think and reflect before moving on to the next chapter. Those pauses will sometimes ask a question of you the reader or allow you to quietly pray in response to what you have read.

May this book inspire you to make each day count. We trust that you will be encouraged to 'seize the day' and in every sense, draw the marrow out of life. Choose wisely friend, live each day with passion, purpose and commitment to the Person and cause of Christ.

Carol and Paul Alexander

Acknowledgements

The accumulated richness of our lives causes us to owe much to so many people. Because of the season in which we have written this book there are some that deserve special recognition. The entire community at Trinity Bible College and Graduate school – students, staff, faculty and so many supporting friends are deeply appreciated. Paul's leadership team have held his arms high through the challenges of building a vibrant College on the northern plains of the United States. Carol's Graduate School team have labored long and hard to help establish masters and doctoral programs that now serve leaders around the world. Despite the many demanding requirements of institutional leadership, they have given us the time and space to write and for that we are grateful.

Dr Dave Garrard graciously edited each chapter as we went along. Years ago, we were given the joy of serving with Dave and his wife Ruth, at Mattersey Hall in England. Sharing a childhood in southern Africa and a missionary call, we had much in common. Dave is a rare individual who has combined a rigorous academic background with unwavering love for God and His work. We are very grateful to him.

As with any of our published works, we acknowledge the commitment and love of our children. Anna and Rich and our two beautiful grandchildren Ava and Ty are consistent in their love and support. Jason is always inquisitive about what we are doing and where we are going. Not a day goes by without us being in touch. Our achievements would be small and our lives anemic if we did not enjoy the relationship that we have with our precious loved ones.

Paul and Carol Alexander

Chapter One

FIRST STEPS TO
OBEDIENCE

. . . .

*There will be no peace in any soul until it
is willing to obey the voice of God.*
DWIGHT L. MOODY

CAROL

Week days had the same familiar rhythm throughout my childhood in
South Africa. A cup of hot tea was served to us in our beds before we
surfaced. Our faithful maid, Johanna, was always first in the kitchen
those early weekday mornings. She would put water in the kettle, and
its whistling sound, as it rose to the boil, would be the first alarm in my
subconscious, sleepy brain that the night had swiftly passed and a new day
was about to begin. I now doubt if any of us four children would have been
willing to face the day without that morning cup of tea. On those cold,
early, winter mornings, that warm liquid would seep through my veins
and give me the strength needed to creep out from under my cosey warm
sheets to confront the challenges of another day.

South African homes were not built for the cold winter months. The
windows are single glazed, most houses were built with brick, and there was
never central heat or air conditioning in our homes. This made the early
winter mornings more challenging and uninviting as the cold air seeped

through the crevices of the windows and into your bones. Houses were built for the summer months and had large porches and big swimming pools for enjoying the summer breezes and cooling off after those blazing hot summer days.

When we eventually shed our pajamas, and put on our attire for the school day, the aroma of egg, bacon, sausage and coffee were a luring invitation to the table. There were those occasions when the rush to get to the food left us with much needed parental intervention in helping adjust our attire. My brother's tie often needed retying, my uneven socks and sometimes shoes, needed changing and our creased blouse or skirt needed a quick iron. Nevertheless, we always managed somehow in those chaotic mornings to get off to school on time.

I often forgot my school lunch on the breakfast table which made for a most miserable day. Watching other children devour their beef and mustard sandwiches, sponge cake, and delicious cool drinks, while my empty belly, watering mouth, parched palate and hungry eyes, looked on in misery. This left me hoping against hope that some generous child would sense my anguish and share their lunch with me. No such child was ever to be found. Such is the way of childhood.

Sundays also had a similar rhythm to them. The day began with breakfast, then church, a roast dinner for lunch, and an afternoon drive with a mandatory stop at the ice-cream shop for a delicious "soft serve 99." For those who do not know what this particular treat is, allow me to inform you. It is, undoubtedly, the creamiest vanilla ice cream in the world; added to this decadence was a flake Cadbury chocolate, which was shoved right into the middle of the cone. This treat necessitated immediate consumption or the vanilla ice-cream started to melt and drip down the side of your thumb, creating a deliciously sticky mess. However, this was seldom an issue, because, as the sweet, creamy, goodness hit your palate your taste buds demanded more gratification, and thus the entire cone was demolished in less than a couple of minutes. Sundays were wonderful days.

Sunday School always started an hour before church and I found that infinitely more palatable than the weekly message from the minister. On one particular Sunday, the teacher informed our class that all children 13 years and older, were invited on a church camp to an area called

Scottburgh, on the Natal coast, now called KwaZulu-Natal. My friend and I were ecstatic at the thought of two weeks at the coast without siblings or parents to interfere or inhibit our lives. I was excited to tell Mom and Dad about the opportunity, and of course, they were delighted for me to go and experience the delights of the ocean and other adventures planned for us.

I have always loved musing and reflecting on God's ways and plans for our lives. It seems to me, that God does some extraordinary things in the cycle of everyday ordinary existence. There are times and seasons where I have been quite unaware of any Divine intervention and yet, as I reflect, there are many of those defining moments that have occurred in the cycle of daily life. This awareness has developed a lifelong pattern for Paul and me. Every morning, we begin our day with prayer and ask God to intervene in our plans and the daily rhythm of life. Without doubt, those prayers have been answered and afforded us opportunities and privileges that have been life enriching. We will share many of those stories in the coming chapters.

This church camp was one such occasion. Little did I realize that a decision I made one starry night, would be my first step of obedience into a life of *radical obedience*. Do I have any regrets, I hear you ask? Not even one. My life, at times, challenging and trying, has been an adventure that if I were to do over again, I would change little. The little that I would change, has had nothing to do with journey on which the Lord has led us. The only changes I would make, would be my desire to yield that stubborn self-will, more readily and easily. This so as to learn quickly the lessons God was trying to teach me and to be prepared to wait more patiently for His perfect timing. On occasions my humanity has got the better of me and still, I find my stubborn self, rearing its ugly head, and hence, I pay the price for such indulgence.

Back to that night where I first encountered the Good News about Jesus. It was a sultry summer evening. Natal can get very humid in the summer and your skin is constantly damp with the thick sea air. The stars were out in all their splendor; there was a light breeze making the leaves on those magnificent pepper trees tremor ever so slightly. It was a perfect January evening in the Southern hemisphere. At the camp, there was joy-filled singing to begin with and lots of rowdy voices chattering between songs. A general air of happiness and laughter filled the canvas tent, that particular evening.

Archie, the camp Director, got up to introduce five or six young people and told us that they were going to give their testimonies. I honestly wondered what on earth that meant. Why did they have to give a testimony, had they committed some wrong? I knew something of court cases and appearances. Nelson Mandela, had become a prominent figure in our nation, and I, along with our parents, followed his trials and knew that he was called upon to testify time and again about his involvement with the ANC (African National Congress). I am simply trying to say that this type of meeting was unfamiliar to me and the only context I had for testifying, was a court of law.

The first young person got up and spoke confidently about inviting Christ to take control of his life. He shared about a peace that he had experienced and the joy of knowing that his life now had a purpose. Others shared along similar lines and one or two also spoke about the added joy of knowing that heaven would be their home one day. I listened with rapt attention. I had never heard anything like this in the church we attended every Sunday. I only remember that the more I heard, the more my heart yearned for this experience. I was captivated, and a desire was pulsing through my veins to know and experience this amazing Jesus of whom they spoke. I only knew and understood God as some transcendent Being, rather distant, somewhat scary, but good and holy. Those two characteristics seemed to evade me in my early years. Good and holy were in my view unattainable and in my parent's opinion, they were probably sorely lacking in me.

I had, as a child, what I might call religious inklings. I hounded my mom with questions about eternity. She had to listen to me day after day, rattling on and on about what happens to our souls when we die. Endless questions about the Bible, God, and eternity must have wearied my poor mother, but she never lost her patience, and in her own way, tried to explain theological truths to me. I know God saw the longing in my heart, and the God shaped vacuum in my soul. I believe as Blaise Pascal said; "There is a God shaped vacuum in the heart of every man which cannot be filled by any created thing." The problem is that human beings often live their lives trying to fill that deep void. Truthfully, nothing will ever fill that gap, no person, no experience, no drug, alcohol or anything else. That specific space is God shaped, and only He can completely fill it. That evening, I was made aware of the hole in my soul, and I instantly responded to the invitation to receive Jesus.

I sat in Archie's tent as he further expounded what it meant to be a true Christ follower. I willingly yielded my heart, soul, and every part of my being to Him, knowing with childlike faith, that He would be with me throughout this journey that I embarked upon that sultry summer night. My first step to a life of *radical obedience* had just begun.

And what a journey it has been. Read on as the story unravels.

PAUL

Mine was a caring home and typical for the post war 1950's and 60's. My Dad, whose parents were Scots immigrants to South Africa, studied to be an accountant, and it prevented him from being conscripted in the early years of World War Two. When he did eventually put on the uniform, he was assigned as a prisoner escort for prisoners of war that were being transported to South Africa, and what was known at the time as Southern Rhodesia. He never spoke much of these experiences but told me one day of their rapid crossing of the southern Atlantic from Cape Town to South America and then how they hugged the coast to avoid any German U-boat activity all the way to New York.

There they loaded personnel and supplies. Their ship was the British ship the Queen Mary and was one of the few that could outpace the German submarines. There was so much loaded into the ship in New York that it bottomed out on the bed of the Hudson River. After off-loading a significant amount of equipment, they sailed into New York Harbor and reloaded by ferrying out the supplies. It is interesting the things we remember from childhood.

My Mom's family line was from a prominent family who were a part of a large British migration to the Eastern Cape in South Africa in 1820. Her Mom was a Londoner who met my grandfather in Guildford, in Surrey, England. My Grandfather had been gassed in the trenches of Normandy in the First World War (winning a medal for bravery) and then sent to

England for rehabilitation. While my grandmother volunteered in the rehabilitation home, she met my grandfather and so my grandparents met, fell in love and eventually married.

So, our home enjoyed strong traditions. Christmas and Easter were always celebrated with familiar rituals. Some of my happiest memories are of Easter egg hunts each year and Christmas lunch with all the important food items, especially the plum pudding that on occasion was brought into the dining room with my older brother playing the bagpipes and piping it in flaming as it burned off the alcohol from a tot of brandy.

Due to our Scots heritage, we were faithful members of St Marks Presbyterian church in Yeoville, Johannesburg, South Africa. It was a grand church for its time with a solid tower at one end and a fine organ. The choir was a key part of congregational worship, though I never had a voice that qualified me to play a part. The church also had a vibrant Sunday School, and I do remember the emphasis on memorizing Bible verses. It was only many years later that I fully appreciated the efforts the Sunday School teachers made and their impact on my life.

These very happy memories were not exactly repeated throughout my schooling. I was bored and unfortunately a little mischievous. Every report I ever had from school ended with comments such as "Paul would do well if only he applied himself" or words to that effect. What I lacked in the classroom I made up in the playground. Later in the day I would catch the bus home and by the time I made my way into the house my school uniform and shoes were off, I was in play clothes and off to another exhilarating afternoon with friends. We played hard! If fact, viewing my childhood through the eyes of a parent I am surprised I survived it. I had to have stitches from wounds on three different occasions and often went to bed with painful sprains.

On one occasion, a close friend, who will reappear in a short while in this story, whispered to me in the classroom. He had brought a bottle of coke to school. He had it in his little backpack. He had run to get the bus and it had been shaken profusely. He had run so as to not be late and it was shaken again. His proposition was that if were to sneak it out when we went to swimming classes that day, he would share it with me. It was impossible to resist. I secured it to my waist using the elasticized belt that was a part of my school uniform and then untucked my shirt to hide the evidence. As I walked calmly and looking most innocent down the corridor the bottle slipped out of my belt. It had been so badly shaken that it exploded as it hit the floor. A large shard of glass flew into the inside of the left thigh missing the artery by a hair's breadth. The teacher nearly fainted, I clutched it to prevent more bleeding and was rushed to a doctor's surgery. After seven stitches and deeply regretting that I never got to savor the delicious drink, life went on.

My friend's name was Chris Carey. He came from a large family that always seemed to be having much more fun than mine. We spent hours together organizing "wars" with neighborhood kids. We would fill a bucket with clay from a nearby stream and then fix fist size dollops to flexible willow branches. When war was declared we would hurl these clay lumps by whipping the willow branches. The clay would fly at great speed and many of the other boys would retreat in tears. I received a few painful welts during these times.

Our fun came to an end as we entered high school and Chris was sent away to boarding school in a town called Grahamstown. We lost contact for almost a year. In early 1969, just before my 14th birthday we reconnected. It was a joy to spend time together again but I immediately sensed something was different. He seemed calmer and more considered. The edginess of an adventurous childhood was not there. I assumed it was just because we were growing up but he soon let me know that things really were different.

His two older brothers had become fervent Christ-followers and their example was so compelling that Chris soon followed. It was not long before he invited me to a church that was only a few blocks from my home.

That Sunday night in late January was an experience that I had never had before. Vibrant singing was followed by people telling their stories (I found out that this was called a testimony) and then an energetic preacher kept our attention for the next thirty minutes. Although this was all strange to me, I never felt awkward but the following minutes were most strange. The preacher asked us to bow our heads and close our eyes. I thought this was prayer, but he kept talking to us. He reminded us of our eternal souls and the need to find Christ as Savior and Lord. I had never before considered that I needed to make this kind of choice or decision.

And it grew stranger yet. After an impassioned appeal the preacher invited those of us who did not know Christ to show our desire to follow him by raising our hands. I immediately decided this was not for me. We were sitting in a balcony on the very last row and I was ready for it all to be over. The next thing I knew I felt a warm hand grasp my wrist and fling my hand into the air. The preacher obviously had good eyes and was keen to have a response and so immediately I heard him say that he had seen my hand. Chris had raised my hand for me. Thinking the ordeal was over I was shocked to hear the preacher now ask all those who had raised their hands to make their way to the front of the church. I was not going to go but Chris had other plans. He quietly rose, continued to grip my wrist and then lead me to the front. I felt it was all a strange dream.

It went from bad to worse. After a few words, none of which I really comprehended I was instructed to follow someone into a side room. I had no idea what was going to transpire. A very kind young man by the name of Costa Mitchell showed me some verses in the Bible and asked if he could lead me in a prayer of repentance and dedication. Hoping it would bring my adventure to an end I responded affirmatively and was duly prayed for. On my way-out people smiled pleasantly at me and a few congratulated me on my decision. By the time I arrived home I was still not so sure what had actually transpired.

One of those who had acknowledged me was a young man, about three or four years older than me who I knew lived just a street away. He invited me to a youth service the following Friday. I agreed to attend and thought about it often in the following days. I even got ready to attend but at the last minute my courage failed me and I turned around and went back into the house. I was settling down to an evening at home when there was a knock on the front door. It was Winton, the young man who had invited me to the youth meeting. He told me how he had looked for me, missed me and then determined to come and find me. I will forever be grateful to Winton but the journey to the service is worth reporting.

Winton was something of a backyard mechanic and he owned a British built Mini Minor Cooper S. It was a very desirable car for a young speedster. He had changed the wheels and had large tires. He had souped up the engine to high performance levels, added an oversized and very noisy exhaust pipe and, just to be sure, had covered the front dashboard with psychedelic faux orange fur.

All I remember was the terrifying speed with which Winton navigated the corners. I became overtly religious praying earnestly, reciting the Lord's prayer and even remembering parts of the Apostles creed. In no time, we were at the church, and I exited that little car grateful that I was still alive.

In the following hours, my life changed. I met authentic young people who wanted nothing else but to follow Christ. I became socially attached, made plans for all night prayer meetings, youth camps and service days. My uncertain experience of the church service the Sunday before made sense. I started reading the Bible and found my whole outlook on life changing.

I knew it was real in the way in which things changed in class. We all had to learn a second language and I hated it. In fact, I had a secret agreement with myself to see how long it would take to reduce the sweet young teacher we had to tears. I would ask ridiculous questions and openly disturb the class. The poor teacher was often exasperated by my behavior and as a result would banish me from the class. I spent most of those classes standing outside the door and hoping that the headmaster was not making his rounds.

A few weeks later I realized that I had not been sent out of the class once. I was learning and my teacher was actually liking me. Eventually it occurred to me that I was changed. I was indeed a new creation, and my own testimony was as valid and real as someone who had been set free from drug or alcohol addiction. In truth, my life was only just beginning.

Prayerful Pause:

Is there a vacuum in your soul? Only God can truly fill that gap. Saint Augustine put it this way; "There is a God-Shaped vacuum in every man that only Christ can fill." The amazing truth is that God will fill every part of the hole as you open your heart and allow Him access into your life. He is there, standing at the entrance to your life, waiting for your response. He will never go where He is not invited. He gave you a free will to make the decision to serve Him or not.

Think carefully, choose wisely, your entire future now and forever depends on this one decision.

If you have been resisting the prods and prompts of God, I am quite certain there is either a restlessness in your soul or deep discontent. Pause now, listen to that still, small voice speaking through these pages and yield to His loving call. If you are a committed Christ follower, pause and thank God for the gift of life and for His salvation.

Chapter Two

OBEDIENCE TO
THE WHISPER

· · · · · · · · · · ·

The cost of obedience is small compared
to the cost of disobedience

AUGUSTINE OF HIPPO

CAROL

Leafing slowly through the pages of my journal, discovering memories hidden beneath the passage of time, infuse me with joyous and grateful recollections. Those memories, hidden for some time in the crevices of my mind, surface to remind me again of how perfect God's plan for my life was, and still is. And so, I recall one eventful night where the still, small, voice of God, spoke loudly into the depths of my soul, and another step to *radical obedience* had to be taken.

I was just 16 years old, and attending Fairview Assembly of God church, in Johannesburg. I was part of the youth group, but happily attended every Sunday service, as well as our weekly prayer meeting, and the Wednesday night Bible study. I loved church.

One early morning, as the sun was pushing through the clouds and bathing my bedroom with light, I heard God speak to me in the stillness of my bedroom. It was a particularly lovely spring day, and the intoxicating fragrances of spring were filtering through the crevices of the windows, filling me with a glorious sense of hope. In that atmosphere of warmth God asked me a question; "Will you serve me?" I did not hesitate; "Yes, Lord, I will go anywhere and do anything you want me to," was my immediate response. I know it might sound odd to say, "God spoke to me", because if we cannot hear an audible voice how do we know it was God who was speaking to us? Could it be my active imagination or are there really occasions where God does speak to us as humans? I know, that some people might say that God only speaks to us through the Bible. However, I will add, that the Bible is full of stories of God speaking to men, women and even children. Perhaps you are thinking; "True, but that was in a bygone era, we have the Bible now and that is all we need." Christians in general, believe that God is a relational God who wants to communicate with His people. I think, a God who communicates with His people, is probably one of the major distinctions between the Christian faith and other faiths. He wants to have a personal relationship with His children. All I can say is that I knew in the depths of my being that on that spring morning, God spoke to me and called me into His service. His voice was not audible but it was a quiet and emphatic voice in the depths of my soul.

Then came the "but!" This is where our doubt always comes in to play. Where the questions begin to arise. And I had three major problems that I felt were a hindrance to God's call on my life. "Lord, you know I cannot sing and I am not musical and I am a girl." I simply could not conceive how God could use this ordinary little South African girl. I had no special talent, no unique ability, no outstanding intellectual capacity, and so, I felt as if I had nothing of worth to offer Jesus, and above all of my contentions, I was a girl!

In the early 70's, women in my denomination, were not regarded as fit, equipped, capable or called to "do ministry." The general assumption was that "woman in ministry" was not a biblical concept. The biblical texts that this doctrine was based upon, were in my view, misunderstood and misinterpreted. Of course, women were permitted to teach Sunday School or go as a missionary to another country. Have you ever stopped to ponder this theology? What does it say about children if women can teach them but not adults? It implies that children are inferior. But, even worse, what does it say about the peoples of other nations that missionaries feel called to go to? Why is it acceptable to teach and minister to African men and women, when that same missionary woman is not permitted to teach those people in her own nation? Are people of other nations inferior? This kind of theology, in my view, lacks a biblical understanding. It diminishes women, relegating them to tasks, that in these peoples limited perspectives are only fit for women. Generally speaking, that implied having babies, keeping the home fires going, attending prayer meetings and knitting socks for missionaries. Thankfully, much has changed since those early days, but to this day, I still encounter men that treat me with disdain, believing I should not be doing what I feel God has clearly asked me to do.

I am aware that women had no status in First Century Palestine. They could not own property, in fact, they were the property of their father or husband. Neither could women own land and they could not testify in a court of law. However, as I have read the biblical narrative and the writings of the apostle Paul, it is clear that Jesus came and restored women in their rightful position. Jesus challenged the prevailing cultural assumptions of racism and sexism and gave women the significance they deserved. One only needs to read John, chapters four and eight, and the story of Martha and Mary, to be persuaded that Jesus valued women as much as men. We are all made in the image of God. God calls women and men. When God gifts a woman, it is no less of a gift than the same gift given to a man. My understanding, as a young person, and this was the teaching I had received, was that unless I could sing or play a musical instrument, I would be useless in God's service. I assume the understanding back then, was that it was reasonable for women to sing theology to people but they could not talk or preach theology. It makes no sense to me.

That night, in the 16th year of my life, God spoke to me and said; "I did not ask you for your talents or your abilities, I asked you for your obedience to walk the path I have ordained for you." From that night on I have never doubted, no, not even for one moment, that the Lord had a work for me to do, and that He would equip me to do whatever He called me to. Of course, I knew it would not involve music! And every church that we led and ministered in can be grateful for that.

Another night, that is indelibly printed in my mind, occurred some months later. I had gone to church this particular Sunday night with my entire family. As usual the singing was vibrant and filled the atmosphere with a palpable joy. Harold Barker, one of the church elders, was leading the singing with his usual enthusiasm. He had a grin that slowly spread across his beaming, round face, and seemed to light up the entire room. His large frame moved back and forth with infectious joy.

I always listened carefully to the message being preached, and on the following day I would go over my notes and reinforce what I had learned from the sermon. After Sunday evening service, tea and coffee were served in the minor hall to the side of the sanctuary. Our family always lingered to engage with our friends and church community.

I had been attending the youth meetings at our church for some months. Paul had been attending the church and youth meetings for quite some time as well. I recall the first time I walked into the youth meeting that he was leading. I was struck by his infectious personality and his passion for Jesus. As a teenager in the 70's it was inappropriate to show any kind of interest in the opposite sex. I was attracted to his infectious smile, blonde hair, and blue eyes. He was also very athletic and was at that time rowing for South African Schools, with the potential of rowing in the Olympics. He was fit, handsome, and had a fine physique. I know he is going to revel in reading this paragraph. I just hope he is as honest as I am about the first time he saw me!

This particular evening, he gravitated towards another girl, a brunette, and he was absorbed in a conversation with her for far too long. I watched on in anguish. What could he possibly like about this girl? And, how inappropriate to talk to her whilst I was standing at the side of the hall sipping my tea trying to make conversation with my friend, but totally distracted at the scene being played out in front of me. Boys! The conversation probably lasted no longer than five minutes, but in my opinion, that was four and a half minutes too long. Paul, fortunately for him, cannot recall the girl or the conversation. However, it distressed me and left me feeling down in the dumps that Sunday evening.

I said little in the car on the drive home. When we arrived home, I went straight to my bedroom and got between my sheets to have a little pity party with the Lord. I told the Lord that I was in love with this boy and could he please comfort my heart and show Paul that if he did like this brunette, he would be making the most terrible mistake of his life. I lay awake for some time, aware that the darkness had a thick, black texture to it. Sleep alluded me. However, eventually I fell into what I believe was a light sleep. I was sleeping but not deeply. I heard a whisper in my subconscious mind; "Carol, Carol." The voice called my name twice. I immediately woke up and knew the Lord was speaking to me, I replied: "Yes, Lord." Then I heard His soft, but clear voice say: "Soon, very soon, Paul will be yours and all yours." Right now, as I sit here, some 52 years later, that memory is as crystal clear to me, as the sound of a bubbling brook and the feeling of fresh mountain air on my skin on a beautiful spring day.

In that moment, I knew, without a shadow of a doubt, that God was letting me know that I would marry Paul. I never had to fear another brunette or blonde or any other girl, because God had ordained that our lives would be joined for His service. It has been a privilege and a blessing to serve God with Paul.

PAUL

The twentieth century presented people of Christian faith many unprecedented challenges. Starting in the early decades of the century the worldview supported by most people who claimed an allegiance to the Christian faith was shattered by World War 1 or what became widely known as the Great War. The nations that had colonized vast areas of the world motivated by a sanctimonious claim of "bringing civilization" to savage peoples, were now demonstrating savagery on the battlefields of the Somme or Passchendaele never seen in human history.

The massive diplomatic failure of the Treaty of Versailles sowed the seeds of Middle East conflict and then later, the combined conflicts of World War 2, the Korean War and the brutal war in Vietnam, all combined to challenge the core of Christian belief, particularly in the West. The Russian Revolution and the rise of classical post-modern philosophy resulted in a divided world, global conflict, student activism and post-colonial political upheaval. This was exactly the world that I was entering as a young teenager towards the close of the 1960's.

I knew little of the Cuban Missile crisis or of the dividing of Korea. The struggles of the Chinese people after the Cultural Revolution were hardly ever mentioned in the world that I inhabited but everyone knew that all was not right. As a young person in South Africa, I was made aware on a daily basis of a growing global antagonism towards the country that was run by an exclusively white minority government. On a very regular basis we were reminded of the need to uphold our "Christian" faith in the face of a titanic struggle between good and evil. Unfortunately, nationalism and Christianity became badly entangled in our society at the time.

Globally evangelical Christians who believed that we should have a personal faith in Christ and confess His Lordship were more convinced than most previous generations that all these global events were signaling the end of the age. The more fervent of these Christian groups had adopted a kind of obsession with the coming of Christ and (maybe even more importantly) the exit of the Church from this evil world. I listened carefully to fiery sermons on how Christ would return as a thief in the night and was consistently warned that even a minor slip in my faith (and legalistic morality) could result in me being left behind.

My formative years of being a Christ follower were a blend of ecstatic worship services, all night prayer meetings, a bold witness of Christ's love for the world and a deep fear of judgement and being somehow excluded from the culmination of history—the exit of the Church from a sick and dying world.

Being a young South African did not help me in managing this dichotomy. The government-controlled media, the education department and fiery political speeches reinforced the communist threat. Books were circulated in our church on the persecution of Christians in the former Eastern bloc. Brother Andrew was fearlessly smuggling Bibles into communist countries. Stories of people being shot to pieces while caught in the barbed wire that made up part of the Berlin wall were graphically reported.

Although our local media suppressed most objective reporting, our newspapers were filled with the Communist threat and especially the activities of so-called Liberation movements that were threatening our way of life. Almost always the final picture was one in which the conflict of faith, freedom and a Judaea/Christian worldview was under immense threat from the evil, anti-God forces of Marxism.

This was my world and context at one of the most impressionable stages of life. I was absolutely certain that I was a changed person, and I had no doubts about being a passionate Christ follower. My challenge was how to live this faith out in an ever increasingly conflicted space. I joined the Christian Association at my school. This seemed to amplify the divisions in our society. Many of my school friends were Jewish and I was aware that some belonged to what we considered to be radicalized families. One good friend was the son of the attorney who was leading the defense of Nelson Mandela and his co-accused in the infamous Rivonia treason trials.

With little meaningful help from my pastors, I was trying to navigate this complex world. It seems to me now that my leaders at the time had a simple theological approach to almost everything. We now call this concept "redemptive lift." In other words, the only responsibility of the Church is to preach the salvation message of Jesus and any transformation—personal, societal or political must be the result of people becoming fully devoted followers of Jesus. Social action, political involvement or even attempts to speak of issues relating to justice were frowned upon.

Saving me from confusion were three anchors for which I will be forever grateful. The first was St Mark's Presbyterian church in Yeoville, a suburb of Johannesburg. Populated by many first-generation Scots immigrants, including my Grandparents, this church was a seedbed of my developing faith. We were encouraged to learn Bible verses by heart every week. Confirmation classes were taken very seriously and the annual calendar including Harvest Festival, the Christmas eve "Nine Lessons and Carols" service and the important Easter weekend services were instrumental in forming some deep inner convictions. The next anchor was a campsite called Rocky Valley. Owned by the Presbyterian Churches of South Africa, this valley in the Magaliesburg Mountains became a haven for me. I volunteered for service camps whenever I could, learned to sing old choruses around a campfire and found a caring community. The third anchor was "Schools and Varsity Camps" organized by Scripture Union.

It was on one of these camps that my sense of the call of God first began to develop. On the Indian Ocean side of the spectacular Cape peninsular is a small valley with a little town at the beach. It is called Glencairn. We would embark by train on the long journey from Johannesburg to Cape Town. Carriages were filled with young teenagers making their way south. The journey required two nights on the train. The food was awful but the company was exuberant.

I clearly recall the pushing and shoving of the carriages in the early hours of the first morning. The electric locomotives were being shunted out of the way and a huge steam locomotive was replacing them. For all the next day, we were pulled through South Africa's stunning landscape by one of these old behemoths. Almost all of us ended up with cinders in our eyes because we insisted on putting our heads out of the windows.

The next morning, we would arrive at a town called Beaufort West. The shunting started all over again, an electric locomotive took over and by mid-morning we were descending through the beautiful Hex River Valley, through the mountains of the Western Cape and into Cape Town. Then we transferred to a local train line and made our way to Glencairn, where we disembarked and walked about half a mile up the little valley. Rows of tents awaited us, and the camp began. Fun, games and practical Bible lessons filled every day.

On the third day, we were leaving the campsite. The path to the beach ran through lush undergrowth and the breakers could be heard in the distance. Despite the anticipation of diving into the beautiful translucent blue waters I felt an overwhelming sense of God's presence. It must be remembered that I had never consciously made a specific commitment of my life to Christ that I described earlier. I was a part of an active church community, but it had never been a personal or specific decision on my part. But this sense on this day was real and a feeling of deep calling to deep welled up within me. Without a word, I let my friends keep walking, and I returned to the camp. There were no words, and I had no idea how to describe what was taking place within me.

Providentially one of the trusted camp leaders saw me. He quickly called me to sit on the edge of a deck that was attached to the main hall. Oh, how special that moment was. When eventually I found a way to explain my feeling, I verbalized my sense of God calling me. I clearly remember saying that I knew that God was calling me, but my dilemma was that I did not know where or to what. Wisely the camp leader assured me that this was how God's call almost always worked. He speaks to the depth of our being and awaits simple and sincere responses. Based on our response God then takes over and through nudges, prompts, whispers and clear signs of His will leads and directs us.

That was enough for me. A short prayer and the reassurance of a wise young leader was all that I needed. I knew God knew best and my heart lightened, my face brightened, and I ran off to enjoy a beach day with my friends.

That moment was catalytic in my life and the whispers of God's call and His will for my life were just beginning. Within a year I had walked down the aisle in that little church with my friend Christopher Carey by my side. A year later I met Carol for the first time. Standing in the entrance to an ancillary building in our church in Johannesburg I glanced to my left and saw the most beautiful head of blonde hair I had ever laid my eyes upon. As Carol turned towards me my heart danced, my teenage feelings erupted and deep down I knew I was in love. It would take some months of carefully planned encounters and desperate efforts to charm this beauty but by the March of my eighteenth year we were holding hands, spending hours on expensive phone calls and deeply in love.

Prayerful Pause:

If you are a young person or even older for that matter, and are sensing the call of God, then our prayer is that this chapter will encourage you to pursue that calling with every fiber of your being. The call of God for ministry is a privilege and an honor. We understand that there are people in ministry that have a different experience to ours. One partner is in ministry and the other has a different calling. We respect that as much as we love the fact that we can share ministry together. Every person is unique and God has different callings on our lives. There is no particular way that is best. We only know that God gives each one of us grace for the race He calls us to run. If you are in ministry and experiencing challenging times, pause and ask God for grace to navigate this season. Please, don't throw in the towel. Ministry is challenging and not for the feint hearted, you need to dig deep and find peace and grace for this specific time in your life.

For those who are feeling that whisper or nudge into ministry, pause and ask God to lead and guide you. Psalm thirty-seven reminds us that our steps are ordered by the Lord. The Lord promises us that even if we stumble or falter, He will uphold us. What a promise! For anyone who has stumbled in their Christian walk, please take courage from this Psalm. Pick yourself up, dust yourself off, and keep on keeping on.

Chapter Three
EARLY ADVENTURES OF OBEDIENCE

· · · · · · · · · ·

To fall in love with God is the greatest romance;
to seek him the greatest adventure; to find
him the greatest human achievement

AUGUSTINE OF HIPPO

PAUL

Some things were easy choices for Carol and me as we began our courtship. For example, attending church was simply not optional. It was not always possible for me because I was in my final year of school and attending every service was a challenge. I loved Carol all the more for her determination to be a part of every possible event at our local church. A form of *radical obedience* was forming.

Although it took a while before our formal courtship commenced, we saw a lot of each other. Carol's home was always open, and her parents were exceptionally hospitable. I took every moment to be with her. At the time, I was excelling in high school athletics rowing for the school's first fours and first eights crews. This took immense amounts of time for training both on water and on land.

The training paid off and at the start of my final year of high school I was invited to participate in selection trials for the national South African Schools rowing team. After a grueling process that involved hours of fitness testing and rowing with several combinations of other rowers, I was selected to row stroke side number 3 for the national side. My parents burst with pride.

I was happy but resented that my additional role involved rowing practice on a Sunday. It was for me a spiritual battle that I asked God to help me navigate through. Although I missed church, I would quickly make my way to Carol's home each Sunday afternoon.

During one of these special days, our youth group decided to spend some time at a local park handing out invitations to an upcoming Billy Graham crusade. We did so with enthusiasm. After handing out the last of the invitations, youthful energy caused me to run down a small bank and playfully tackle a friend to the ground.

He was stronger than me and responded by trying to cut my legs out from under me. The way he did this caught my foot and I heard something that sounded like a pistol shot snap in my ankle. I bravely tried to stand but fell forward in great pain. All the tendons down the outside of my left ankle had snapped. With national rowing championships fast approaching my parents took me to see the best orthopedic surgeon they could find. It was to no avail; a plaster cast was applied, and my rowing career was over.

Strangely, I was not disappointed. For one thing, it enabled me to volunteer to serve at a children's camp that I knew Carol was also serving at. Well, that time away cemented our relationship. Romantic walks were accompanied by the loud noise of my cast stomping along. But this began the early expressions of our *radical obedience.*

Our church had a connection to a remote mission station in the southern Maluti mountains of the little kingdom of Lesotho. Mt Tabor, had been established by Swiss Pentecostal missionaries and we fell in love with those serving there. David and Gretchen Kast would be very instrumental in my developing sense of the call of God. Every school holiday I would make my way across the border at a little town called Wepener and make the trip to this wonderful but faraway place.

I became fully committed to the concept of Christian mission as I saw the sacrifice and commitment of these amazing people. There were many political factions amongst the Basotho people, and these would sometimes erupt into fights. The next day those suffering from brutal machete wounds would find their way to Mt Tabor where these gracious missionaries would care for them. Others came to have rotten teeth extracted. With no anesthetic but with a steady hand Gretchen would yank out the offending teeth.

One day David asked me if I would take one of the horses and ride across the mountains to a trading store about a two-hour ride away. He wanted me to fetch a bull as they were hoping that their cows would have calves. I set off all alone. Children would run out of huts and welcome me. I was the first white person many of them had ever seen.

Eventually I rounded a corner overlooking a deep gorge where a mountain stream flowed. The trading station was remote and was a relic of a colonial age. The homestead was surrounded by a covered porch and the whole house was set in immaculately manicured gardens. The red corrugated roof stood out starkly in comparison to the thatched huts I had seen on my ride across. The little picket gate had a latticed archway covered over with beautiful white climbing roses. Despite its remoteness it was an idyllic scene.

I tied the horse to the fence post, brushed myself down and approached the front door. I had remembered to ask the trader if I could lead his bull back to Mt Tabor to service the cows there. This was all a most wonderful adventure for a city boy. I knocked on the door, stood to my full height and waited.

You can imagine my surprise when a rather attractive young lady about my age answered the door. To add to my surprise, she was dressed in her pajamas. I gasped and she shrieked. I stumbled for words, and she excitedly told me that she had not expected to see me at the door. I said something similar and with a blushing face I said something like I would come back later. With huge relief she shut the door, and I ran back down the path, through the gate and mounted the horse in a hurry.

I can hardly remember the ride back to Mt Tabor. The horse knew the paths and we arrived back safely. David came out of the mission house looking in every direction for the bull. He finally asked me where it was. It was only then that it dawned on me that I had not succeeded in the mission I had been sent on. They sent someone else to fetch the bull later

22

that week and in all the years following David has never ceased to remind me of my failed venture.

Mt Tabor and its dedicated missionaries deeply impacted my life. I knew that Christian missions was a part of my future. That has proven to be the case.

Carol and I volunteered to serve at a Vacation Bible School for children. It was held in a small church in a part of our home city that was known for its poor housing and generally poorer population. We had an amazing time and as the week came to a close, we both agreed that continuing the good work was essential. It was not long before we decided to start a Good News club for the many kids we had come to know.

We approached the pastor of the church thinking he would be quick to accept our enthusiastic offer. He informed us in no uncertain terms that he did not want the carpet of his church spoiled by children and that the building would not be available for a Saturday Good News Club. His response proved to be the first but certainly not the last response by short sighted Christian leaders that would baffle and amaze us.

Undeterred we looked for an alternative venue. Driving up the road where the church was located, we noticed a simple house that was built above a fairly large garage. We stopped the car, walked up the stairs at the side of the house and knocked on the door. An Asian man answered the door and when we explained what we were hoping to do we found out that he was a committed Christian. He ran a small printing press in his garage but offered to rearrange things and we could use the space available. We were ecstatic. Our pastor's wife gave us a carpet. We made a flannel board which was the digital equivalent way of telling Bible stories to children at that time. Carol signed up for a course offered by an organization called Child Evangelism Fellowship. We gave most of our small salaries at the time to buying resources. Most Thursday nights were taken up making visuals and preparing materials.

The children found out and the first Saturday morning we had so many children that the garage was filled and the driveway had to contain the overflow. We began to visit the homes of the children that attended. I remember visiting a 5-year-old child in his home. The family had an ancient washing machine made from galvanized iron. One day the mother was drunk. She locked the little boy out of the house, pulled the electric plug out of one side of the machine and placed the live end on top of the machine and went to the front of the house to have another drink. The child managed to open the window and crawl inside. As he was letting himself down, he landed on the machine which gave him a huge 220-volt shock. Fortunately, he was thrown clear by the shock, but he came very close to being electrocuted. On another occasion, the woman locked this same little boy outside the garden and left him on the sidewalk. The terrified five-year-old tried to get in by climbing the cast iron fence. As he maneuvered his legs across the top he slipped and was impaled in his armpit by one of the spikes. Neighbors responded to his screams, and he was rushed to hospital for stitches while his mother remained drunk in the house. These situations disturbed us and we tried to engage with the families in meaningful ways.

We began to visit the family on a weekly basis. During those times, we would go and sit with this precious little boy and pray with him before he was put to bed. His father was grateful. His siblings loved us being in their home. Layer by layer the lives of service that we would live for the next fifty plus years were taking shape. The early adventures of faith were coalescing into a pattern. Loving Jesus and serving his people would define the rest of our lives.

It so happened that at the time these early adventures of faith and obedience were transpiring in our lives our church extended an invitation to a young British couple to serve as pastors. Brian and Josie Downward arrived in South Africa after completing Bible College and traveling around the world. I was immediately impacted by Brian's preaching. He was masterful at the use of illustrations and some of his stories caught and held my attention like no other preacher ever had. They also sang together, and church became engaging making us not want to miss a single service.

All too soon the eighteen months of their commitment came to an end and they were embarking on their return to England. Typically, Carol's parents' home was the venue for one of the farewells. As Brian left their home that evening, he did a most unusual thing. He looked at us, found a piece of paper, wrote something on it and then said that if ever we felt led to go to Bible College that we should reach out to the address on the paper.

The college he was recommending was the British Assembly of God Bible College. At that time, it was situated in a leafy suburb south east of London called Kenley. Our relationship had developed to the point that we spent every minute we could together and often would spend hours in conversation about the will of God. We also spontaneously prayed together.

I cannot recall exactly when or how the decision was made but we were soon committed to going to Bible College in a faraway land. Neither of us had ever left the country before, we were still in our late teens but a sense of *radical obedience* was already being entrenched in our lives. We filled out the application forms and then waited in keen anticipation for a response.

Unbeknown to us the college was in the middle of a move to a campus in the north of England. Our applications must have been caught up in the move and so we waited for what seemed like an eternity. It was certainly several months but our enthusiasm, prayer and expectation was never diminished. Eventually the response came. We found out that we had been accepted to attend college.

In preparation for our studies, we both got jobs. Carol worked for an insurance company in central Johannesburg. My Dad was a certified public accountant, and I was able to get a job with an accounting firm. My job took me to many places in the area as part of an audit team. Whenever I was in the home office Carol and I would meet in the library gardens in central Johannesburg for lunch. We made it our aim to each speak to at least one person about the love of Jesus. And we did! In fact, we spoke to many people during those lunch times. We were fearless in our witness to the love of Christ.

Carol started typing lessons in preparation for her studies and the many letters she would write, and we both started saving every penny from our meagre earnings. Buying our suitcases for our big trip was in and of itself an adventure. Hers was an expandable brown one and mine a soft sided green. Every purchase and every step of the journey was filled with excitement and anticipation for our future.

Then we were presented with a somewhat unusual fact. Our friends who had been so instrumental in our decision to go to England, wrote to inform us that the rules at the Bible College were strict and did not allow couples to be in a relationship. The only way to get around this was to be engaged. The excitement of our lives at the time had never allowed us to give thought to this and we were both too young to have seriously considered it.

I arrived at Carol's house one evening to some conspiracy of which I was unaware. Carol's siblings had decided to assist me in asking my future father-in-law for his daughter's hand in marriage. They virtually pushed me down the passage where I knocked on the bedroom door. He was about to get ready for bed but invited me in and somehow, I managed to get a garbled collection of sentences out of my mouth asking if Carol and I could be engaged. To my amazement he agreed, and I left the room and walked back down the passage with my head held high.

We chose a not too costly ring out of a jeweler's window that Carol loved. Every penny was being put aside to aid us in our future studies and so a diamond was not in the offing. The jeweler informed us that the stone was a golden topaz however, we discovered later that it was just a piece of colored glass. She still treasured the ring because it was a declaration of our deep love and commitment to each other. We were finally engaged and Bible College bound.

The months flew by and the big day for our departure finally arrived. We had bought very cost-effective tickets that took us via Luxemburg. In a daze of emotion, we said our goodbyes and took our seats. As I was seated, I looked up and saw a familiar face. It was a school friend of mine. In fact, he had taken my place in the national rowing crew after I had injured my ankle. With surprise, I greeted him and asked where he was going. He told me that by taking my place he had been able to continue his rowing and had now been selected to represent South Africa at the European championships. That we were on exactly the same plane immediately impacted me. I was heading to Bible College with my fiancé, he was going to a rowing championship. With a huge lump in my throat, I held Carol's hand and quietly admitted that God was somehow at work and His plans for our lives were so much bigger than we could ever imagine. The adventure of *radical obedience* was continuing.

Prayerful Pause:

If you have been apprehensive in your Christian journey, we encourage you to pause here for a while. It is true that a life of *radical obedience* can be challenging. However, life is fraught with obstacles all along the way. The only pathway to peace is the path to obedience. It is radical because it does not come naturally to any of us. We are prone to put confidence in our own abilities most times. It is only when the situation becomes bleak that some pause to ask for God's help. But, what if, you could live in a constant place of trust? Proverbs 3: 4-6 tell us to trust in the Lord with all our heart and not to lean on our own understanding; and if we submit to Him, then He will make our paths straight. This calls for a *radical obedience.* You might be thinking: "I do not have this level of faith." All you need is faith to live the life that God has mapped out for you. Our stories are our unique journey and we had to walk the road God mapped out for us. You cannot run our race and we cannot run your race. What we can assure you of, is that God has mapped out your race and He will give you the grace to run your race. Trust him my friend. The path to *radical obedience* is the best possible one for you.

Chapter Four

REASSURING OBEDIENCE

· · · · · · · · · ·

The driver on the road is not safe when he
reads the signs, but when he obeys them
AIDEN WILSON TOZER

CAROL

Both Paul and I had experienced the call of God on our lives and we both knew that it was a call to full time service. I remember feeling overwhelmed with a sense of privilege that God would choose to use me as one of His instruments. I knew I had no extraordinary gifts or abilities and I was acutely aware of my humanity, faults and failures. Yet, despite this God was calling me into His service.

Paul and I started courting when I was 16 and he had just turned 18. Our love for each other was propelled by our love for God and our joint call to serve Him. We were both attending Fairview Assembly of God church in Johannesburg. It was a great mother church and had been founded and pastored by the late Fred Mullen. When we attended the church the youth group was thriving and the young people were hungry for God. It was a vibrant atmosphere for my faith and spiritual growth.

Like a parched desert drinking in those early summer rains my soul was thirsty for God. I was deeply invested in the church and can remember going to the prayer meeting on Tuesday, the Bible study on Thursday,

Youth group on Friday, Saturday evening Bible studies in our home, and then church twice on a Sunday. I was awash with love for God and His word and I was totally invested in His service.

Dad had renovated our home and had turned our huge double garage into a family room for his children to entertain their friends. My parents were incredibly generous in hospitality and there was never a week end where our home was not alive with young people. It was not uncommon to have 30 to 40 young people for lunch on a Sunday and the door was always open for the stranger. I am so grateful that I was nurtured in an environment like this.

At the time Paul and I began attending the church we had a pastor from England, who served in the church for just over a year. On his final evening, before returning to the UK, we had a meeting in our home to bid him farewell. As he left that evening, he said in passing; "If anyone is considering going to Bible College, I am leaving the address of the one I attended." That throw away sentence caught my attention and held me captive in its grip. God does work in strange ways. I know that Paul felt the same pull as I did and we shared our feelings with each other. Yes, we were young and we were both in Matric doing our final year of schooling, but we had a strong sense that this tug in our hearts was God nudging us towards His will.

Armed with the knowledge that we were meant for each other and that we would be married one day, we began praying fervently for God to reveal His will to us. We both wrote to the Assemblies of God Bible College in Kenley and waited anxiously for a reply from them. Paul phoned me a number of weeks later his voice laced with excitement as he told me that he had just received his letter of acceptance from the College. I was happy for him but disappointed that I had not heard from them and wondered what would happen if I was not accepted. Would Paul go without me?

In the days that followed despair clung to me like a heavy cloud diffusing me with anxiety. The thought occurred to me that perhaps God did not have a purpose for my life after all. We humans are prone to doubt and I was allowing negativity to invade my soul. Our thoughts can sometimes become so bleak it is as if charcoal clouds gather in the depths of our soul bringing a deluge that drowns out all hope. Yes, that was me.

I had heard and felt God's call but now the doubts were flooding every part of my being.

I came home from school on a Thursday afternoon still feeling dismal and downcast. Mom handed me a letter from the Bible College. I took it cautiously and retreated to the solace of my bedroom. My hand was trembling as I held that letter. I must have stared at it for almost five minutes before I gained the courage to open it. I read the words slowly and deliberately that I had been accepted as a student to Kenley Bible College. Slowly sunlight crept into my soul again and I felt as if all the intoxicating fragrances of spring were filtering through the window of my soul. I simply sprayed the air with a volley of praise that reached mom in the kitchen. The next call I made was to Paul to tell him that we would be going to Bible College together.

By the time we left for Bible College they had relocated to Mattersey in Doncaster. That in itself is a long story that our friend Dr William Kay has written about in his book *Inside Story*. It is not our story to tell. We bid family and friends farewell at Jan Smuts airport on the 5th August 1974. It was a blustery winter day with the buttery dust from the old gold mines blowing fine powder to bid us farewell. Little did we imagine the journey we were starting and where it would lead.

The future was waiting for us. We would ride different waves in different seasons. There would be waves of hope that would ride high for seasons and then the waves of challenge that would dump us leaving us tossed about and feeling as if our dreams were shattered. But through it all we would always pick ourselves up from that disastrous wave and not allow hope to be washed out. We determined from the outset that anger and bitterness were not options for us. When difficulties, unfairness and inequity play out anger often lurks in our souls and then bitterness can follow quickly on its heels. We have tried to deal quickly with those emotions knowing full well that they are like a cancer in your soul. Once that cancer gets root in your soul it is the beginning of spiritual death.

And so, our journey together began. Leaving South Africa, and the comforts of home has not always been easy but we both saw it as an exciting adventure and engaged it with the enthusiasm of youth. We had both grown up in middle class homes. My dad was a business man and I grew up never wanting for anything. Paul had a similar childhood where neither of us ever experienced want. So, arriving at Bible College in the early 70's had some surprises in store for us.

The Second World War had ended in 1945, but Britain was still experiencing political and economic turmoil in the 70's. I recall high inflation, unemployment and endless strikes in the nation at this time. From a political and social perspective, it felt like the winter of discontent. The College was in a tenuous financial position, of which we would later in our lives (when we led the College in the late 90's) know the full extent of those difficult years. I shared a dormitory with six other girls and my first real shock came when I had to fill out the roster for my bath night. I was told to choose one night in seven to take my turn to bath. I cannot remember what I said but I was flabbergasted that we were not allowed to have a daily bath. I had grown up in a home where daily bathing was not a luxury but a necessity. I must note here that I had to continuously work on my attitude which at times could be quite negative. I was learning so many lessons along the way. It was also the first time I had encountered another culture and had to realize that there were no right or wrong cultures they were merely different. My worldview began to expand and as it grew so did my Christian values.

The food we ate was below par and I recall that during our time at Bible College we were never served one piece of fruit. In our second year, Paul got really ill and when the doctor saw him, he had a raging temperature of 102 degrees. He was diagnosed with trench mouth. The doctor informed him that it was from malnutrition and dirty utensils. The weather was also a challenge after the glorious Johannesburg summers. The wind often blew so hard that it whipped laundry off the line. The cold would creep through the crevices of our windows and dominate the room with a frigid air. The curtains often blew in the breeze that was coming through the cracks in the walls and windows.

With all the challenges of drafty and freezing cold bedrooms, limited baths, and poor food we had two wonderful years. We made lifelong friendships and learnt more in those few years than we had in all the years growing up in comfort and plenty. Hardships can be good for the soul. We also learned to walk a pathway of obedience and trust. We were beginning the journey to *radical obedience.*

Every weekend the College sent us out on ministry trips. This afforded us the opportunity to preach and do children's work. Paul and I got deeply involved in our community and started a Good News Club for the children in Mattersey. We also loved traveling and preaching and meeting different people. As I reflect now, I am grateful for the many opportunities I had as a woman to preach in different churches. There were many people who did not believe that woman could preach or teach, but at our College woman were given all the same opportunities as men. This was back in the 70's, so it is significant that our movement was beginning to make way for women in ministry. I am profoundly grateful for those early opportunities that came my way to develop my own gift, passion and calling.

When we were out on ministry weekends, we would stay in people's homes which was always interesting. There were times that we were accommodated in a lovely warm home and then there were other times. You can use your imagination. Like the time we had finished dinner and the plates were collected and promptly placed on the floor for the cat to lick after which the dessert was served off of the cleanly licked plates. I could write another book!

I do remember one occasion that built my faith and taught me a lesson. My good friend Joanna and I were staying in the home of a medical doctor. They served us tea which was accompanied with lots of delicious eats. This was one of the joys of travel as we were afforded some good food in many of the homes. We often had a delicious roast dinner and decadent desserts and cakes. The medical doctor and his wife went out of their way to host us and make us comfortable. We spent the evenings sharing stories and telling of all the exciting things God was doing in our lives.

I heard the beckoning sound of the kettle whistling in the kitchen and so I went through to spend a few moments with my hosts while Joanna was getting ready. It was a cold and dull morning as the sun struggled to peek through the clouds. The only light in the room was a lone lamp in the corner that seemed to fill the room with a lovely peachy glow making it feel cozy and warm. The doctor poured me a steaming hot cup of tea and as the delicious amber liquid quenched my parched throat they began to speak in a whisper.

The doctor and his wife told me that they felt God wanted them to pay for all my school fees for the full duration of my time at Mattersey. I was flabbergasted. This was the first time in my life I had ever had anyone apart from my parents offer to do something like this for me. I am not sure if my response was the right one, but it was honest and the only response I knew to give. I told them I was overawed at their offer but that my parents were covering all my costs. They looked disappointed but left the topic and the remainder of the day we had with them was wonderful. However, when I told my pastor of the generous offer that had been made to me his response surprised me. He told me I should never turn down an offer for help. He said; "You robbed those people of a blessing." I said; "But I only told them the truth which is that my parents are paying all my fees." His response was; "Well, it would have given you the opportunity to pay for someone else who had a need." I am still not sure how I would have navigated that particular offer with absolute integrity but I know that from that day onwards I had a deep sense that God would care for Paul and me. That He would meet all our needs and provide for us. There are many stories to share in the coming pages but that lesson that day was foundational for me. God would care for me and if we ever had more than we needed then it would afford us the opportunity to give to others.

Prayerful Pause:

Obedience is at one and the same time simple and complex. I think the complexity comes from our own humanity. We often take the simple things of God and complicate them. To walk by faith is actually simple. I am so grateful for my Bible College years where I learned trust and obedience in ways that I would never have learned elsewhere. Sometimes the most difficult times are the ones that produce the most fruit.

If you are reading this and struggling with your walk of faith and finding the pathway of obedience a challenge to navigate, I hope that this chapter has encouraged you. God is a good God of that you can be certain. He is never out to trick you in any way or to play around with you and your feelings. God is a loving heavenly Father. It is true that circumstances do not always go the way we planned or desired, but if we honor God He will order our steps. We may not understand why we have encountered challenges and trials but one day everything will make sense. There have been challenging times in our lives where things went quite differently to the way we anticipated. Years later, as we reflected, we could understand more fully and appreciate that our prayer had not been answered the way we had prayed. There are some things we still do not fully understand but I do know that eternity will make sense of them.

If you are going through a challenging time, I urge you to pause, reflect and seek to understand the lesson God is trying to teach you. He only has good plans for His children.

Chapter Five

LEARNING OBEDIENCE
TOGETHER

. . . .

God provides the wind, man must raise the sail

AUGUSTINE OF HIPPO

PAUL

As our time at Bible College began drawing to a close, the obvious question of what would we do next was foremost in our minds. We resorted to the well-tried disciplines of praying and on occasion we fasted as well. Should we return to South Africa? We gave this serious consideration but, as I will record at the end of this chapter, other opportunities presented themselves.

Getting married was the first priority. By this stage we had been engaged for two years and it felt like we had already lived out a huge amount of our lives together. We had traveled to churches almost every weekend to serve and often to preach. We had continued our ministry to children and had started another Good News Club. This time it was held in a minute old Primitive Methodist Chapel in our village. Nevertheless, we packed thirty to forty children in each week. Stories, crafts, singing and prayer were always included.

We had no doubt that our relationship was to be for the rest of our lives. We loved each other deeply and we shared a passionate commitment to God and His work. Realizing that most of our friendships were those we had developed in England we decided that we should be married there. My parents were not really pleased about this but gave us their blessing and go ahead. Typically, Carol's parents immediately planned how they could make it the best imaginable day for us.

We made big plans, especially considering the small and parochial village in which we had lived for two years. The Anglican church in the village was an ancient Norman building dating from the late 12th century. Unfortunately, there were bats in the bell tower and so we found out that the bells could not be rung on our wedding day. The local vicar was a kind man and supported us when we asked to use the church. By church law he had to lead us in our vows and have us sign the register but gave us freedom to plan all the rest of the event as we would have it.

Carol chose her best friend Joanna as one of her bridesmaids. Joanna had come to college from Afghanistan where her parents were missionaries. She and Carol had become the best of friends. One day a message arrived and Joanna was asked to leave the lecture hall. She received the tragic news of her brother's death in an accident in Pakistan. This tragedy brought Carol and Joanna even closer together and so when the wedding was being planned, she was an obvious choice. Her other bridesmaids were her older sister Gaille and her younger sister Tracy.

I chose my roommate Ian Green to be my best man. Ian came from south Wales and had a marvelous story of finding Christ and experiencing dramatic changes in his life. Our room was a small one and so we knew each other well. I later was honored to be Ian's best man and we have enjoyed a lifelong friendship. My younger brother-in-law Geoff was also in my wedding party along with Gaille's husband Vaughn.

The planning for our wedding was intense. Carol's Mom was six thousand miles away, she had no other family nearby and we were used to working off the very limited funds we had during our college years. She shone! Carol found the materials for the dress she wanted, found someone to bake a cake and decorate it with South Africa's national flower, the Protea and then set about organizing a reception like our little village had never experienced.

About ten days before the wedding Carol's family flew in from South Africa. Her Dad had sent an amount of money to us so that we could buy them a car that would help the family to get around the UK. I found one in a nearby town. It was an old Ford, Zephyr six, and fire truck red. You couldn't miss it! Carol's sister and her husband had arrived a few days prior to her parents and younger siblings. The morning arrived for us to go and fetch the family from Heathrow. My brother-in-law, Vaughn and I left early in the morning that they arrived to ensure that we made the three-hour journey to Heathrow, London's airport, in good time to welcome the family. It went relatively smoothly until about twenty miles from the airport. It was unusually hot, and the traffic began to back up. We crawled along knowing that the family had landed and were probably wondering why we were not there. There were no cell phones in those days and there was simply no way to contact the family and warn them of our delay.

We finally were within the airport property. For those that are familiar with Heathrow, it is approached by a fairly long tunnel. We entered thinking that it would only be a few more minutes and we would be reunited with our loved ones. Halfway through the tunnel the engine cut out and the car stopped almost immediately. People who had already spent hours in traffic were most upset. Within a minute a tow truck was in front of us, told me to let off the break and steer behind them. Putting a rope around the front bumper (it was real metal in those days) they yanked us out of the tunnel and deposited us in a side alley. No further help was available.

Vaughn ran to the terminal and found the family. My future father-in-law was most irate because they had been waiting for hours not knowing where we were or what had happened. I was spared his wrath because I was trying to work out what to do with a broken-down car. We called a taxi who took the family to a church nearby. We had wonderful friends there who helped arrange transport for them. It took me three days to get the car out of Heathrow and to a mechanic for repair.

My future father-in-law forgave me once he comprehended the situation and all was soon forgiven. The big day that we had been planning and longing for arrived.

We had dear friends from South Normanton, a town not too far from the College, who had lived and ministered in South Africa for several years. They arranged for a sheep to be slaughtered and for a butcher in Derbyshire to make pounds and pounds of "boerewors"—a favorite sausage of all South Africans. Fires were started ready for the grilling of all the meat. Carol's parents had brought suitcases filled with pineapples and avocado pears both of which were still not freely available in England in the 70's. Our college and our village had never seen such a feast. We pitched a huge tent and decorated it beautifully. All this took place on the lawn in front of our college. It was the first time in two years that we had seen so much meat and fruit and vegetables. Carol's Dad was extremely generous and did not hold back ensuring the best steak, lamb chops and salads were on the menu.

We had a local lady bring Carol and her dad to the church in the quaintest horse and trap. They trotted out of the long college driveway, around the village and pulled up in front of the ancient church. I was waiting with my friends at the front of the church. It was an ideal setting. As Carol entered the church on her dad's arm my heart pounded and every emotion you read about in romantic novels flooded my mind. My sweet bride was making her way down the aisle for us to say, "I do" for the rest of our lives.

There was one regrettable incident on our special day. After feasting, saying speeches and enjoying one of the warmest summer days on record Carol retreated to her room to change in preparation for our short trip to a nearby hotel for the first night of our honeymoon. Again, she was absolutely beautiful, and we made our way to our very old car that had served us so well during our college years. We knew immediately that something was wrong. Some of our mischievous college friends had set out to tie cans to the back of the car and write "just married" on the windows but some of them had just gone too far. They had found a mature manure heap nearby and for some unknown reason piled spade fills of the smelly stuff into the car. They tied an overlarge can to the back of the car and as I backed out it dug into the ground and the top end bent the gas tank reducing its capacity by nearly half.

We gagged our way to the hotel and tried to make light of it. The next day I returned to the college to try and clean the car. The carpets were beyond repair, and I had to rip them out. We found butter smeared on all the handles and that alone took ages to clean. The gas tank never was repaired but we ran out of gas on our honeymoon because I never could know exactly how much gas we had.

We had reservations in a simple little Christian hotel in north Wales. It was more like a boarding house but we were married and ecstatically happy. Those days flew by in a haze as we celebrated our love and marriage.

A few weeks later we bade farewell to our parents and our global pilgrimage began. This was *radical obedience* in a primitive but very real expression. As a result of our commitment to student ministry during our college years we had received an invitation to conduct a series of services in a small church in Aberdeen, Scotland. The pastor and his wife lived in a city home built of traditional grey granite. Aberdeen is often referred to as the "granite city." Miraculously the church had been able to purchase an elegant building that had previously served a Presbyterian congregation.

The beautiful church now housed a struggling group of intrepid Pentecostal people numbering less than thirty. We were accommodated in the attic of the pastor's house and preached every night for a week. During the day, we handed out invitations and encouraged people to attend. That same church is now led by some of our dearest friends and serves several thousand every weekend. They eventually bought the largest conference center in the region. The growth of the church had nothing to do with us but we are so glad to be able to remember some small seeds that were sown. Our deepest convictions were slowly cementing themselves into our lives forming foundations for decades of leadership.

As our time in Aberdeen came to a close, we received an invitation to serve a church in Belfast, Northern Island. We drove our old blue Cortina across the beautiful center of Scotland and caught a ferry to the Emerald Isle. Belfast was still in the grip of terrible sectarian violence. Whole portions of the city were cordoned off and there was a huge police presence. We nervously made our way through multiple police roadblocks to our host's home.

The divisions in the city are difficult to describe. Catholic inhabitants lived mainly in the Falls Road area and a large wall had been erected to keep them from their Protestant neighbors. Car bombs, attacks on restaurants, and other violence took place almost daily. At least sixty years of tension had built ever since the Easter uprising on April 24th, 1916. This had occurred in Dublin and ultimately resulted in six counties being formed into Northern Ireland which then remained as a part of the United Kingdom. The Irish Republican Army had launched one terror attack after the other to try to force unification. By the mid to late 70's this conflict and tension still held this beautiful island and its lovely people in its grip.

We learnt that the church where we were to preach was located on the Shankill Road, the heart of militant Protestant Unionists. We could hear gunfire most evenings. A few days into our stay the church organized an open-air meeting on a prominent corner about halfway up the Shankill Road. There were several notorious drinking houses (called pubs) in the immediate area. The Brown Bear pub was a well-known hang out for a murderous gang who became known as the Shankill Butchers. Everywhere there were reminders that this area was ravished by poverty, crime and political violence. Our host church bravely served in this very hostile environment.

We set up a small public-address system and then hoped to gather a crowd by singing some Christian songs. As we got started, we became aware that there was something happening at the city end of the Shankill Road. Some ran to find out and came rushing back with the news that hundreds and possibly thousands of women were gathering for a historic peace march. Crowds began to gather. We shared testimonies and I was asked to preach a short message on the saving work of Christ. Soon the police arrived in armored Land Rovers and asked us to move on.

We were happy to comply as we knew several hundred had already heard our message. Just as we began to pack up a TV news crew arrived and asked if they could film what we were doing. I preached again, this time in front of the cameras. It turned out to be a news crew from the Republic of Ireland and I have been told that some footage of our open-air meeting found its way on to the main newscast that night.

The atmosphere was electric. People feared an outburst of violence but crowds of women marched on. Amongst them were nuns from Irish convents. This was perhaps the first presence of Catholic people on the Shankill Road in decades. The crowd moved towards the park at the end of the road. Thousands marched and we felt privileged to have witnessed one of the largest peace initiatives in the long and sad struggle of these beautiful emerald isles.

Our adventures in Ireland were not over. We managed to fit in a few days in the west of the country before arriving in Dublin at the invitation of a dear pastoral couple by the name Jim and Viv McGlade. This was long before the European Union was formed, and Ireland was generally still a poor country and Catholicism was deeply entrenched. There were a number of militant Catholic organizations, and they made it their duty to make life difficult for any non-Catholic group.

As a result, the little church that the McGlade's led was in the basement of a city tenement building. As we arrived at their home, Viv came running down the pathway to ask us to drive immediately to the YMCA building in the city. Her husband Jim needed out support.

We arrived at the foreboding stone building and made our way to the basement. Jim was sitting exhausted in a far corner and opposite him was a disheveled, desperate looking man. Throughout our young Christian lives we had been reminded from time to time about the struggle between light and dark. We had heard about demon activity but it was clear to me within seconds that this man was not simply mentally ill. He had glazed eyes, spit ran through his unkempt beard, and he looked tragically sad.

He was indeed demon possessed in exactly the same way as passages in the New Testament talk about people who Jesus set free. We agreed that we should try to get the poor man to the church facility. I sat at the back of the car with him. Twice he opened the car door as we were driving through town and attempted to step out. I reached across and pulled him back into the car. For several hours, we prayed with him and commanded the demons to leave him. It all seemed to be to no avail. Several hours after midnight I felt my heart and mind open up. I would call it now a revelation. I had an overwhelming sense of the authority of the name of Jesus. In a whisper, I looked into his hurting eyes and commanded the demons to leave him. He fell backwards and an eerie sound seemed to rumble from deep within him and then circle around the building. As certainly as I know my own heart I knew this was real and that God had prevailed over evil. He lay still and at peace for the first time in years.

I remember leaving the little basement church in the early hours of the morning. Exhausted, I supported myself by leaning against a parking meter. I recall the fearful sense that I had actually heard cries of *hades* in that horrible encounter over the previous hours. I prayed a simple yet profoundly heartfelt prayer. I told God that I had heard the cries of a lost eternity. I then asked Him to do with me what he may, send me where He will but to please use me to save others from ever having to utter that same cry.

This was another step in our journey of *radical obedience*. The journey was only beginning but it was proving to be eventful in every sense. We left Ireland by ferry to Holyhead in the north of Wales. Soon we would be making our way across the ocean to Brooklyn, New York.

The foundations of a life lived in obedience to Jesus were being laid. One experience after the other was adding to the base on which we would build our future. We were madly in love, just married and felt an overwhelming sense of privilege to be in the service of a gracious and loving God.

Prayerful Pause:

In a quiet and contemplative moment, we would urge you, our reader, to consider the journey of life and especially the formative experiences that you have had. This could very easily be painful, but it is necessary. Some of those experiences need a redemptive grace that brings healing and removes the pain. Ask God to do this for you. There could be some of you that need help to realign your life. Simply ask God to help you. He is listening to the cry of your heart and He will be quick to respond. Did you veer off the pathway at some point? If so, make some good decisions and recommit your life to God and let Him know of your desire for *radical obedience*. There may be those of you who simply want to pause and return gratitude to God. Thank Him for His reassurance and the grateful memories you can reflect upon. Celebrate the goodness of a gracious God in quiet and heartfelt worship.

Chapter Six

SIMPLE OBEDIENCE

· · · · · · · · · · ·

Give your life to God;
He can do more with it than you can

DWIGHT L MOODY

CAROL

Living and working at Teen Challenge, Brooklyn, New York was enriching but sometimes felt like being on a railroad track. One side of the track was invigorating and exciting, while the other side was challenging and stretching. Life seems to be like those two sides of the track. One aspect of our lives can be demanding and the other side can be thrilling. That certainly defined our time in Brooklyn.

I remember being utterly mesmerized and awed by the city when we got there. There were economic challenges that you could not only sense but see. I remember staying on 444 Clinton Ave in an apartment building owned by Teen Challenge. What stunned me was looking out of our window and seeing other apartment buildings burning. There was also a lot of crime and social disorder was everywhere evident. Additionally, there was much poverty. I remember going for a stroll down Atlantic Avenue with Paul when we first arrived. When we told the Teen Challenge team that we had walked down the avenue they forbade us from ever doing that again. That was enough for me to know that we had to be careful in this beautiful city in which we felt called to work. It certainly was not a safe city back in the 70's.

We reveled in our time at Teen Challenge. Paul and I ran a children's club and Paul also did Bible studies with the men going through rehabilitation. We saw many lives changed but we also saw some of the men go back into their former lives and that was always a heart sore for us. We were only at Teen Challenge for a three-month window and then we started traveling around the United States in earnest.

Here is how we did it.

While we were at Teen Challenge we had no income whatsoever. We were living completely by faith. If this sounds foreign to you then let me simply say it was a new experience for us too. However, our early Christian walk had been forged in the Assembly of God Bible College in the UK, and that is where we learned that living by faith was common to many people in ministry and would be the hallmark of our lives and ministry into the future.

As the weather began to turn in New York, Paul became acutely aware that I was not adequately clad for the icy winter months that were rapidly approaching. As a new husband, he was feeling a sense of responsibility for me and ensuring I was properly cared for. I did not know that he was really praying that he could buy me a coat and boots to navigate the freezing weather. One day an envelope was slipped under our door and in that envelope, was enough money for me to purchase a beautiful winter coat and warm fleece lined boots.

We had a number of preaching opportunities afforded us in Pennsylvania, and we were planning to go there as soon as we had finished our work in New York. We began to pray for a car so that we could get around the States. I remember saying to Paul with real conviction one day; "Well, if we do not get a car we cannot go and preach anywhere." Paul's smile morphed into an expression of alarm as if the lack of a car could possibly hinder God's purposes for our lives.

It was a dreary cold day in New York, the skies were dismal, the wind was blowing and snow was falling steadily on the ground. We drove in the Teen Challenge mini bus to a church in Brooklyn that icy cold Sunday morning. As we got out the van, wrapped in our winter coats the wind was blowing so ferociously that it almost impeded our movements. Those icy arctic winds can chill you to the very bone. We eventually defied the wind and entered the sanctuary to the vibrant worship and singing of the congregation. Like daylight breaking through the charcoal night, the atmosphere warmed our hearts and settled our spirits. We found our seats and settled down to listen to the weekly sermon.

The Pastor got up to speak, he paused, gazed fixedly at the congregation and then pointed his finger seemingly right at me, sitting in the balcony and said; "Don't you ever say we will not go here or there if we do not have a car. If God has called you to go, even if you have to go on a bicycle you need to obey." His words hit me like a slap in the face. How did he know what I had said to Paul in the privacy of our bedroom? My soul felt as if it was stripped bare. God was seeking to show me the layers of selfishness, pride and control that were still a part of the fabric of my being. Was I willing to shed those aspects of my humanity that were hindering my walk with Him? I felt exposed before God as He revealed my needy soul and asked me to trust Him completely. As I bowed my head, acknowledging that God had spoken directly to me through a man I barely knew, I committed myself to *radical obedience* and trust in a God who cared enough to speak to me personally. That was undoubtedly a defining moment in my early life.

We were privileged to preach a series of messages in Stone church New York just prior to leaving Teen Challenge. God was opening amazing doors for us to preach and minister and this was no insignificant invite for two young people. I remember we received a gift from the church of two hundred and fifty dollars for our week of services. That was the largest sum of money we had ever seen. We felt incredibly rich and also encouraged that perhaps we could buy that car that we had hoped for.

We had made some wonderful friends during our months at Teen Challenge. Amongst the many were three young men from Bethany Fellowship Bible College. We forged a special friendship with them during our time there and enjoyed some wonderful week ends away together where we laughed, prayed and ate good food. They were anxious to hear about our time in Stone church and we excitedly told them that we now had enough money, in fact 250 dollars, to buy a car. They all roared with laughter and assured us that we would not be able to buy a bicycle for that amount of money in New York. Determined to obey God, we booked bus tickets for Pennsylvania, armed with the certain knowledge that if we were to preach around the United States, we would probably have to cycle or bus our way around that nation. A car seemed outside of the realm of possibility.

Our first stop was at Teen Challenge in Rehrersburg, Pennsylvania. We stayed with a wonderful couple in their trailer home. The weather was brutal and snow was heavily laden on the ground. Paul and I were not accustomed to snow. Yes, we had lived in England and the weather there is dull, grey and rainy, but we never saw much snow. In New York and Pennsylvania, we became accustomed to the perpetual wind, cold and snow of the northern climes. We loved the snow and had some fun adventures tobogganing and learning to navigate our way to church through snow drifts.

We were sitting at the breakfast table with our hosts indulging in food that we considered treats not breakfast. In South Africa, we ate egg and bacon or porridge and toast for breakfast. We soon learned to revel in pancakes and syrup and decadent cinnamon rolls to begin our day. Those were considered rare treats in our homeland and were quickly becoming standard fare of the day in the United States. As we spoke our host told us that there was an auto dealer just a few blocks away and he was sure that we could find a good deal on a car if we inquired.

We were a little apprehensive as we contemplated previous discussions about buying an automobile, but we made our way to the dealer later that morning. The snow had been steadily and consistently falling all morning. We got to the dealer and asked him if he had any cars for sale. We did not dare whisper the amount of money we had in our pockets for fear that we would be scolded and sent on our way. The dealer said; "There is a 62 Chrysler over there on the right, go take a look at it. It is under snow, so if it starts you can be sure it is a good car." We are not particularly apt to trust a car dealer but we made our way over to the direction he pointed us. Paul started to sweep the heavy layers of snow off the car to discover an apple green colored Chrysler. He thought it was marvelous. I thought it was hideous. It was like a tank and all I wanted was a small, feminine looking car, preferably pink in color.

Paul climbed excitedly into the front seat his face etched with anticipation. He put the key in the ignition, turned it and the engine roared to life. He looked at me, a smile spread across his beaming face and he said; "I am going to buy this little beauty." I had very little knowledge about cars, I only knew that in my eyes, it was an ugly vehicle that would be somewhat embarrassing to drive, but armed with little other knowledge I bowed to his decision and we went to negotiate a deal with the owner. This was going to be awkward!

Paul smiled and cleared his throat. One of the unique aspects of Paul's personality is that when he gets embarrassed, he takes off his spectacles, wipes his eyes and then slowly puts his spectacles back on his face. He did this slowly and deliberately. He looked up at the owner and asked: "How much do you want for the car?" The owner did not flinch when he replied: "Three hundred and fifty dollars." Paul coughed, he took off his specs, wiped his eyes, put them back slowly and said: "I don't have three hundred and fifty dollars." The owner said; "Then you won't be buying this car, will you?" Sometimes Paul surprises himself because he replied with confidence; "I want this car and I am prepared to give you two hundred and fifty dollars in cash." The way Paul spat out that sentence you would have thought we were doing the owner the greatest favor of the month. And the most surprising part of it all was that the owner actually fell for it and said; "Well, you are a lovely young couple and I would love to help you." And so, we bought a 62, apple green Chrysler, the ugliest car we have ever owned.

That car took us all the way around the United States driving over fifteen thousand miles. The only negative was when we discovered after a few days that we had a gas guzzler. The car was gulping gas down quicker than a thirsty baby drinking it's morning bottle. One day Paul looked at me and said; "We are just not going to be able to afford the gas for this car." I had learned a valuable lesson in the church in Brooklyn that cold wintery day. I looked at Paul and said; "Let's pray that God will miraculously heal our car and give us many more miles to the gallon. We were only getting ten miles to the gallon up to this point. Paul looked at me with the kind of empathy you have for a small child. "Go ahead, you pray" he quipped. So, with simple childlike faith, with my hands laid on the dashboard, I prayed; "Lord, we really want to serve you. We have so many opportunities to preach your Word around this nation and we need you to touch our car and give us better gas mileage. Touch this car in Jesus Name." I understand if you, like Paul, think this was simplistic because it was. But I prayed that prayer with faith that God was listening and He would hear me. Would it surprise you to hear that from that moment on, until we sold our car a year later, we got eighteen miles to the gallon. When we sold our car a year later, we sold it for three hundred and fifty dollars, the amount the dealer said the car was still worth.

Oh, the joys of *radical obedience.* We were experiencing answers to our prayers as we walked a life of faith. We were preaching around the United States and seeing God bless us and provide for us in remarkable ways. To save money when we traveled, we would buy bread and cheese and eat it in the car. I looked at Paul one day and said; "Just because we are living a faith life, doesn't mean we need to lack etiquette." He asked me what I meant. "Well, we are breaking cheese with our bare hands and eating like cowboys." His reply vexed me. "No one can see us," he quipped. "But we can see each other and it's disgusting eating like cowboys. I am going to pray that God gives us a knife and fork." I was convinced our parents would not be impressed by our lack of decorum. "Go ahead and pray my darling" was Paul's amused reply. So, I did! "God please give us a knife and fork so we can eat our food with decorum, in Jesus' name Amen." I heard a mumbled "Amen."

We were staying with a couple back in Pennsylvania while on our way to Canada to preach. They were a lovely elderly couple who shared some heart wrenching stories of loss. Two of their daughters had died in road accidents and their hope in eternity and the resurrection were inspiring. We had a wonderful evening with them and headed out early the next morning. As Paul was reversing out the driveway the man started waving his hands to stop us from proceeding. Paul applied the brakes and waited. He ran to the car and said; "Please wait I want to give you something." He came panting back to the car holding two sets of silverware in his hands. He had a knife, a fork and a spoon for each one of us.

As a couple, we were learning to pray about every aspect of our lives. We were invited to preach in a wonderful church in Wilkes-Barre, Pennsylvania with Pastors Ken and Gloria Kashner. Those were wonderful days of sharing stories with each other and having our faith strengthened. We enjoyed preaching in their church and learned so much from them.

Paul and I did not have scarves or gloves at this time. We had never owned them because we had never really needed them before. We had warm coats and boots but we had to keep our hands in our pockets to keep them warm. As with everything we prayed God would meet our need. Just prior to our service on one of the evenings, Pastor Ken called us into his office because someone had left something for us. On his desk were two parcels. One was addressed to Paul and the other to Carol. The card read; "From Jesus." We were overwhelmed to discover that there were a pair of gloves and a scarf for each of us. We were seeing God meet all of our needs.

When we were in Minnesota we stayed with some good friends. We had the privilege of speaking in a number of university chapels, including North Central University, and Bethany Fellowship now called Bethany Global University. The College was deeply committed to training and sending out missionaries. The staff and faculty lived on the campus and shared a common purse. We had a wonderful few days, and their hospitality and welcome was generous and kind.

We were sitting with a couple one evening, sharing all our stories of faith. Paul and I had a particular need about which we were praying. We always determined not to make our personal needs known as we never wanted to appear to be begging. However, I confess that I sometimes try to assist the Lord in His work. My mind starts going and I get some marvelous ideas and recommend them to Jesus. I tend to want to remind Him of who I reckon He could use to meet our needs. Of course, it is usually a suggestion of a person with ample resources. I have always felt that I have given the Lord some excellent recommendations; however, the Lord has never taken me up on any of them. Why? Because He is infinitely wiser than I am. The book of Isaiah, in the Old Testament, tells us that God's ways and thoughts are superior to ours. Those are my words and translation but I think I make the point. So, as we were sitting sipping coffee, Vic turned to his wife Ruth and said; "Ruth, are you thinking what I am thinking?" He whispered in her ear and she nodded and smiled. I can still see the picture clearly in my mind. Vic, got up and walked over to a little dresser. He opened the drawer and pulled out an envelope. He passed it to Paul and said that they had been saving this money for some time and asked God to whom they should give it, and they both felt certain that God had told them to give the money to us. When we opened that envelope, it was exactly what we needed for the next leg of our journey. God never fails and doesn't need our prompting.

We also preached in a little church with a wonderful family called the Peters. The parents were leading the church and were welcoming and kind to us. Their three sons, around our ages were musical and involved in the church. They invited us to preach for a number of weeks and we had amazing services. It was a small but lively community and we had a wonderful time with them and forged a link over the next few years.

One of the memorable stops we had was in Conrad, Iowa, where we were hosted by Pastor Ron and Irma Mooberry. They had a small country church with a congregation of no more than 60 people. It was in this rural setting that Paul and I discovered the joy of family. No, not blood relatives, but the family of God who embraced us and loved us. Our apple green Chrysler by this time had driven thousands of miles and we were in dire need of new tires. As per usual we whispered our prayer to God. The next morning, we awoke to discover all four of our wheels gone. We were distraught and thought rural America was more dangerous than New York city. We discovered a few hours later that two couples had decided to buy new tires for our car. The church in Conrad, and those precious people were family to us and over many years kept contact with us; they often sent us generous parcels in the mail, which always seemed to come at precisely the right moment. One of the wonderful aspects of our time in Conrad, was that it was the first time in our married lives that we were hosted in a little cottage, and we were all alone. We had slept in other people's homes, in lounges, on floors, on camping beds but we had never in the first two years of marriage been completely on our own. We reveled in those few weeks.

On one occasion, I recall we were in need of gas and we did not have any money. It was a particularly cold morning and so I asked Paul to get my coat for me. We only travelled with two suitcases. One had our winter clothing in it and the other our summer clothing. The winter suitcase had not been opened for quite some time. Paul got my coat out for me and I was grateful for the warmth it provided. I put my hands in my pockets to keep them warm and felt something in the pocket. I pulled it out to find an envelope. I opened it quickly to see what was inside. To my delight there was a 10-dollar bill that our hosts had put in my coat pocket some six months previously. I often pause to think about these miracles. God ensured that I only found that envelope when we needed it for gas. It had been in my coat pocket all that time but when we were in want, God revealed it.

I have often said, if you cannot trust God for the small things, how will you ever trust him for the big things. To this day I revel in the little miracles as much as the big miracles. A miracle is a miracle. Whether you are healed from a headache or from cancer it is both the same. I recall one of the seemingly insignificant miracles of our lives. When we were flying to Brooklyn, New York, the airlines provided us with a little pouch containing soap, a small tube of moisturizing cream, a toothbrush with a small tube of toothpaste. We saved the toothpaste and placed it in our bath bag. As I said previously, we had no income and were living by faith. We used that small tube of toothpaste for three months. We were not even aware of the fact that the toothpaste just seemed to be lasting. When we received our first gift of money, I noted our toothpaste was finished. I then realized that God had made that toothpaste last for a ridiculous amount of time. So, trusting for toothpaste, a coat and boots, a knife and fork, a car, gas for our car, and ultimately for buildings, our faith was expanding and enabling us to rest in the fact that God would care for us. *Radical obedience* was the essential fabric of our lives.

Prayerful Pause:

You may be wondering how you can develop and forge a life of trust and obedience. Start today with a simple prayer. Ask God to help you along the journey.

Some of you may have heard of the French man, Charles Blondin, a 19th century acrobat; famous for his tightrope act crossing the 1,100 feet Niagara Gorge on a tightrope. In 1860, a Royal party from Britain saw Blondin cross the tightrope on stilts. Once he had accomplished this feat he was blindfolded and crossed the tightrope without sight. After that he stopped halfway and cooked and ate an omelet. Next, he wheeled a wheelbarrow from one side to the other, and returned with a sack of potatoes in it. Then Blondin approached the Royal party. He asked the

Duke of Newcastle, "do you believe I could take a man across the tightrope in this wheelbarrow?" The Duke said, "Yes!" But declined the challenge.

How often are we willing to get into the wheelbarrow and allow God to take control? I think many of us make that first step in our desire to be obedient. However, when things get tough, when the situation becomes intolerable, we tend to jump out of the wheelbarrow, ask God to step aside and we take control.

Paul and I believe that the way to nurture your trust and obedience is through daily devotions. To read God's word and pray daily will infuse your soul with courage and strength. Build the fabric of your life layer by layer. Prayer, reading God's word, reading stories of the saints who have gone before, regular fellowship with God's people, commitment to your own local church are all ways in which you can strengthen your faith and walk in the path of *radical obedience*. Pause right now and ask God to help you to start the journey or continue your walk of trust and obedience.

Chapter Seven

CROSSING THE PACIFIC–
SCARY OBEDIENCE

· · · · · · · · · · ·

God doesn't expect the impossible from us. He
wants us to expect the impossible from Him!
DWIGHT L. MOODY

PAUL

We concluded our travels across the US and Canada in a place called
Mill Valley, California. It is a delightful town just north of the Golden
Gate Bridge. Our dearest friends David and Gretchen Kast, from our
times in Lesotho were pastoring a small church while David completed
a Doctorate at Golden Gate Seminary. As we had discovered universally
on our faith travels, they like so many others were kind and hospitable.
Multiple small offerings had enabled us to consider where we should go in
order to continue our adventure. Selling our old car for more than what
we bought it for further helped.

Conversations some months before, while we were briefly in Springfield,
Missouri and meeting the General Superintendent of the Assemblies of
God, had led us to believe that our next ministry assignment was Hawaii.
Of course, we were excited, and this was confirmed by a welcome letter
from the District Superintendent in Hawaii. We took all that we had and

bought an air ticket to Honolulu. True to his word, the Superintendent was at the airport to meet us.

But, at that point all our excitement quickly evaporated. He told us that he had booked us into a hotel at our own expense. There was no opportunity for ministry in any church and that his responsibility towards us was now over. We sat in the lonely room not sure what our net move was to be. We certainly were not able to carry the cost of an expensive hotel let alone meals and other costs.

After a while we decided to make the most of it and made our way to Waikiki beach. After plunging into the warm waters of the Pacific we returned to our hotel to consider the next step. I found a telephone book in the hotel room and, knowing each call would cost more than we could afford, I nevertheless began to call the numbers in the list. Some of those we spoke to were dismissive (understandably) but the fourth or fifth person sounded quite enthusiastic. He explained that the church had a little apartment that we would be welcome to use and that his church would be happy to have us preach the following Sunday. Even better, he could collect us within the hour.

Fortunately, the expensive Honolulu hotel was understanding and did not charge us anything as we checked out. We made our way around Diamond Head and into the interior of the island. Within a short time, we were being shown around the small apartment that would be our home for a month. It was certainly not luxurious and was showing signs of damp and mold, but it was a place to sleep, and we were ecstatic that this door had opened.

We ended up being very busy in ministry. By this time Carol had become a proficient ventriloquist, and I managed to play three chords on an eight-string ukulele. We were invited onto the US Naval base for services, youth groups invited us, and we found an opening to preach each of the Sundays.

The first week we were there we followed a pattern that we had developed and kept whenever we were able to. We spent the Wednesday of the week in prayer and fasting. Often, I would find an adjacent room and after an hour or two we would meet together to share what we had felt led to pray about and any other thing we felt God might be speaking about to us. I was not good at this discipline. I started feeling hungry the day before we even started. My mind would imagine exotic meals and I was glad at the end of each of those times of prayer and fasting. But I certainly prayed earnestly in between hunger cramps.

There are some things that are hard to explain either logically or even theologically. One of these is the leading and voice of God. I have concluded that the only explanation is that I know, because I know, because I know. Ultimately this satisfies me and helps me radically obey the promptings and nudging of a gracious and sovereign God.

As I was imagining a meal at the end of our day of prayer and fasting and intermittently praying for God's plan and will to be made known I had a distinct sense that God wanted us to go to Samoa. I had not even heard of Samoa and so let the prompt go by quickly. The same sense came again throughout the morning. By our midday break I reported to Carol what I had sensed. As always, Carol's first response (from then until the present) was to show complete willingness to explore what God wanted for us. I love her and respect her deeply for her unwavering courage and willingness to obey. Perhaps this is really what *radical obedience* is.

The next day we walked into the nearby town and found the local library. In the reference section, there was a gigantic Reader's Digest world atlas. Nervously we opened to the index pages to explore whether there was a place somewhere on the planet called Samoa. To our delight we found it, took note of the grid reference and then opened to the correct page. It was still hard to find. In fact, there are several small islands. One is an American territory called American Samoa. The other islands are independent and called Western Samoa.

Finding the islands increased our excitement and later that day in an unplanned conversation with our host pastor we shared what had transpired. His face lit up and he told us that he knew a missionary in American Samoa. We were enjoying a very fruitful ministry time and he felt sure that his missionary friend would love to have us support them as well. He found a name and address and wrote them down for us.

Our children have no idea of the challenges we faced in communication. We had to write a letter, place it in an envelope, walk to a nearby post office, get it weighed and stamped and then send it off, hoping for the best that it would arrive. Life went on with multiple ministry opportunities. Often people would place a few small notes in our hands and bit by bit these accumulated. About three weeks later there was a knock at the door and the pastor handed us a letter with a broad smile. It was post-marked Pago Pago, American Samoa.

We had already developed a little tradition. Important news of any kind needed a cup of tea, preferably some chocolate and a quiet place to contemplate. We withdrew to our small apartment. After making a cup of tea and opening a precious bar of chocolate we opened the letter with huge anticipation.

As we opened the page, we knew immediately all was not well. In fact, the opening line of the letter was a bold "Who do you think you are?" It then went on to scold us about wanting a trip to the tropical island for ulterior motives and that although we had offered to conduct children's and youth activities and ministry, we were certainly not welcome and please would we stay away.

We were shocked. Neither of us could speak. It felt like someone had slapped us across the face and we were devastated. Inevitably we took the blame and presumed in our innocence and youth that we had not heard the voice of God after all. It was back to routine—and our discipline of prayer and fasting once a week.

Before continuing with the story, I do want to record that we made a decision accompanied by deep conviction that day. We determined that never would we treat young people rudely or with disdain. I believe we have held to that to this day.

As I prayed in the damp little room in that apartment the next Wednesday, I had the exact same impression. I could not escape a consistent prompt to go to Samoa. By the end of the week we were persuaded that God wanted us to go there.

We took the accumulation of small bank notes that we had saved over the month in Hawaii and found a local travel agent. Somewhere in our long-term thoughts we had planned to go to New Zealand. A letter had been forwarded and finally caught up to us in which the Executive Council of the New Zealand Assemblies of God extended an invitation for us to spend several months there ministering across both islands. More about this later.

We discovered that we could buy an air ticket that provided several stops across the Pacific Ocean Islands terminating in Auckland, New

Zealand. Wonderfully we found out that Pago Pago was one of those stops. We bought the ticket and handed over virtually every cent we had.

With complete abandon, we left Honolulu and boarded the flight to Pago Pago. It had hardly occurred to us that we had no contacts in Samoa and there was no money left over for accommodation. This reality started to settle as we made the long flight across the Pacific. To make things worse we calculated that we were arriving at close to 2.00 am in the morning. We felt very vulnerable and uncertain.

We arrived and made our way to a very small terminal. A few young ladies welcomed us with a dance but they looked so tired at that time of the day. We were on a small island one mile wide and twenty-seven miles long in the middle of the Pacific. We knew no one and none knew us. Even worse, we had no funds for hotels or other accommodation. This was scary but felt like *radical obedience*.

As we exited the little terminal in the very early hours of the morning I noticed a bus. All we possessed in the world was two small suitcases. We also had a back pack containing our trusty old manual typewriter in one compartment and Carol's ventriloquial puppet in the other. I had no idea where the bus was going but could just about afford the small fee and hoped that the journey might get us through until dawn. I deposited our cases in the baggage compartment under the bus and made my way to sit next to Carol who had already found a seat.

As I sat down, Carol looked at me intently and asked if I had noticed a couple who had been standing in the small crowd welcoming incoming passengers. I was not sure that I had. She then brilliantly explained to me that I should go and ask them who they were waiting for. I still was not sure who she was referring to but she went on to say that even if I made a fool of myself, it would not matter as we would never see them again. As a naïve young husband, I believed her.

I alighted from the bus, walked back to the crowd that had still not dispersed and guessed at the couple Carol was referring to. Rather nervously I walked up to these complete strangers and asked them who they were waiting for. You can imagine my amazement when they said that they were waiting for some people called Paul and Carol Alexander. Almost lost for words I excitedly told them that we were the Alexanders. They looked me up and down and said that I did not look like what they had anticipated. I never did find out what their thoughts were or what they imagined we might look like.

I asked them to wait right where they were and rushed back to the bus. I told Carol how glad I was that I had obeyed the Lord and gone to speak to them. We hurriedly got off the bus, asked for a refund and retrieved our small bags. The couple had a small pick-up truck. Carol squeezed into the front, and I sat with the bags in the back as we made our way over the rough road that led to the main road that crossed the island. We arrived at their home at about 3.30am and they showed us a little bedroom. They said they would explain everything the next day.

I could not wait that long. I asked what had made them come to the airport and how they even knew that we were coming. They gave into our insistence and quietly shared what had transpired.

This sweet and humble couple served as missionaries on the island under the auspices of Youth with a Mission (YWAM). They had managed to find a small property and ran a Christian bookshop. The island's Christian population was largely a part of the Congregationalist church. This was the result of some extraordinary missionary activity in the mid 1880's. Over the years the churches gained social and even political influence but had become increasingly nominal in their confessional positions. This young couple had tried on numerous occasions to gain some kind of influence in the network of churches that spanned the island.

Some weeks before our arrival they were surprised by a visit from the Superintendent of the Congregational Churches. He and his wife had driven around the island to visit the little bookshop. After a while they explained the real purpose of their visit. They were there to ask if the missionaries knew how to provide for youth and children's ministry in their church and others like theirs. They were desperate for help as they felt they were losing an entire generation of younger people.

Our friend's hearts sank. This was the open door they had wanted but they knew that they did not have the resources or gifts to help. They assured the Samoan couple that they would join them in prayer for this need.

Only a few days later they needed to go to the main post office in Pago Pago. As they were climbing the stairs to the post office they noticed another missionary. They had some minor acquaintance with him but on this day, he appeared most irate. As they ascended the stairs this missionary descended whilst shaking a letter in his hand and complaining about what he had obviously just read. The letter was from "Paul and Carol Alexander who want to serve in children's and youth ministry." He said our names several times along with our stated goal of serving in children's and youth ministry. As he got to the bottom of the stairs, he said that he was going to tell us not to bother coming.

Our new friends drove back to their little apartment above the bookshop and wondered just who Paul and Carol might be. They sounded like the very people that their island's churches were looking for.

In what they described as a profound encounter with the Holy Spirit they felt strongly led to drive to the airport to meet a flight arriving in the early hours of the morning. They had no idea what this couple looked like or who they were. And so, it was that we met them and finally laid our heads down in the back bedroom of their little apartment.

The next day they drove us to the large church just up the hill from the harbor in Pago Pago. We were greeted by Fiti and Savali Sunea. Fiti, was the pastor of the church and the Superintendent for all the Congregational churches on the island. They welcomed us into their simple home and laid out a plan for us to conduct children's services very early each morning before school started. Additionally, we were asked to lead youth services each evening. By the end of the week the crowds of children and youth were filling the large hall in the church. On occasions the children would start singing outside our window at 5.00 am.

Soon we were preaching in nearly each of the churches on the island. Each service was accompanied by mountains of food, especially taro root.

After about three weeks the time for our departure was drawing near. Our friends asked to do our laundry. The problem was it was not returned to us for several days. We found out afterwards that they had used our clothes to make patterns for new ones that they sewed. On our final evening, we were presented with a set of new clothes made with material that was distinctly patterned with South Pacific motifs. What a time. We have thought through our Pacific adventures over and over again through the ensuing years. The entire experience was in every respect *radical obedience,* but we have never regretted those months. God was forging our lives on the anvil of His will, and we could never deny His goodness and faithfulness.

Prayerful Pause:

This is a moment when we, with the benefit of reflection over many years, would now urge you to consider two things. Firstly, if there has been a disappointment in your discovery of the will of God, ask for grace to keep moving forward. An unkind word or like us a letter closing a door, can never hinder the plans that God has for your life as long as you remain committed to *radical obedience.* The second pause we encourage for you is to recognize what we would call the Gifts of the Holy Spirit and their influence on your life. Our friends in Samoa undoubtedly experienced a word of knowledge. It resulted in them meeting a faith-filled couple after midnight on a small Pacific island and then opening doors to an amazing season of fruitfulness. How can the Holy Spirit speak to you?

Chapter Eight

OBEDIENCE IS NOT GLAMOROUS

· · · · · · · · · ·

Hold everything earthly with a loose hand, but
grasp eternal things with a death-like grip

CHARLES SPURGEON

CAROL

As our time in Hawaii and Samoa concluded, we made our way to Fiji. Ministry is not always easy and at times our comfort levels were tested. We were staying with some missionaries in their simple abode. We were always grateful for the accommodation people gave us and because of the generosity we were shown, we have always opened our home to others. Theirs was a very basic structure with no modern amenities and it was sparsely furnished, but it was a place to lay our heads. The gracious missionaries hosted us in their guest bedroom which was small but adequate. There was no air conditioning but we had become accustomed to extreme weather so we never complained. However, I do recall sleeping on the most uncomfortable bed I have ever slept on. I soon learned that the missionary had made the beds himself and I can assure you he was no carpenter. His skills were sorely lacking, and my back ached for a long time after those few weeks. I recall that in the time we spent in Fiji, Paul and I had very little sleep but it certainly increased our prayer life.

When we left the missionaries, we booked a bus back to the capital Suva in order to fly to the next destination on the following day. The missionary had recommended the bus and because it was reasonably priced we readily agreed. I can honestly say that bus ride was memorable for all the wrong reasons.

There were chickens flying around the bus and one almost attempted to roost in my hair. I screamed so loud the chicken instantly departed to look for another poor soul to torment. If we weren't shooing chickens away then we were shooing flies.

We drove on dusty roads, littered with bottles, cans and yellowed newspapers. We passed simple homes with their yellow lawns burnt by the sun's harsh rays and the serious lack of moisture. The oppressive heat washed over our tired bodies with sweat pouring down our frames. Sticky droplets ran down my neck making my hair cling to my skin. Sweat glistened on Paul's forehead as we tried hopelessly to fan ourselves with our hands. There were no windows on the bus just big gaping big holes that enabled the heat and humidity to drench our bodies. As my blouse clung tenaciously to my skin and the sweat rolled down my legs I remember thinking that life can be tough, but I was still so thankful I had "decided to follow Jesus," and with those words echoing in my heart I silently sang; "no turning back, no turning back." I would push on, no matter what!

That bus drive continued to be a nightmare for the next number of hours. Little children, shabby and smelly, their small heads infested with hidden, preying lice, were crying loudly, and many of them were vomiting in the heat. The stench was so powerful that it floated like a noxious cloud. I thought I would be the next to throw up and contribute to the potent odor. Fortunately, the journey ended and we got off the bus just thankful we were still in one piece.

As evening closed, and sunshine faded, bringing with it a charcoal darkness that settled gloomily over us as we made our way to the little hotel that the missionaries had recommended. It was dismal. I needed to shower, but the tub was so filthy I had to keep my sandals on to ensure I didn't end up catching some awful disease. When we got into the bed, the sheets, which I assumed were once white, now had a distinctly yellowish color and stale, damp odor. There were holes and tears in different places, and it seemed apparent that they had not been washed since the last guests had been there.

We were both so exhausted that we fell asleep quickly. We needed to rest because we had to get up early the next morning to walk to the bus stop and catch our bus to the airport for our onward flight to New Zealand. We set our little green alarm clock to wake us up at 4.00am for the long walk to the bus stop. Unfortunately, we had miscalculated how long the walk would take with two heavy suitcases, a type writer, a ventriloquial doll in a separate case, and my purse. We were traveling with all our earthly possessions.

Thankfully, when we commit our way to the Lord He sees what we do not see and I can only think God had our backs. We began walking and Paul quickly realized that at the pace we were moving we were definitely going to miss our bus ride and ultimately our flight. He kept urging me to walk faster. I generally walk quickly, but with all our luggage I was moving at a snail's pace and all the self-will and determination was inadequate. We were simply going to miss our bus and our flight. There was no way around it.

Suddenly, almost as if out of the blue, three very large Fijian people appeared. They asked us if they could help us carry our luggage. I was slightly reticent as I thought their motives may be wrong. However, the weight of our burden was so heavy we put our luggage down and thanked them. They put the cases on their heads and carried everything. We simply floated behind them all the way to the bus stop. As we arrived the bus driver was loading the final piece of luggage into the back and was ready to be on his way. The timing was impeccable. The three Fijians put our luggage down and when we turned around to say thank you they had disappeared. I thought they had vaporized because honestly, they were nowhere to be seen. I now know beyond a shadow of a doubt that Jesus sent angels to help us. I am not sure what your theology is regarding angels, but I do know that God sent us help that early morning because without those three Fijians helping us we would never have arrived at the bus terminal in time. Psalm 91 is one of the psalms that speak to us about the protection of God. It assures us that God will send His angels to guard us in our ways. I do believe that God sent angelic assistance on that particular day.

Our journey to the airport was filled with a deep gratitude. We were ready for our onward flight and the next adventures God had for us.

I am jumping a few years ahead now but I want to share a life lesson I have learned when circumstances are not optimal and can even be described as tough and seemingly impossible. I have, throughout my walk with Jesus, pondered the challenges of life and tried to reflect and learn from them. As I ponder my journey, I can honestly say that it was always in the valley that my spiritual life and my walk with the Lord grew. Don't get me wrong; I do not pray for trials, but when I go through them, I cast myself on God, in ways that I do not when things are going well. In those times, I cling to God like a child folding its arms around their daddy's neck and nestling their head on his shoulder.

It reminds me of a time when our little girl was only 2 years old and her baby brother was a mere 6 months. Paul was a Chaplain in the military during the trying years of the Angolan bush war. I won't share details here because Paul will be telling the full story in a later chapter. We were separated for many months and it was a challenging time for me as a young mother with 2 tiny babies at home.

One day, Paul phoned me and surprised me with the news that the following day, which was a Saturday, the platoon were granted permission to see their families. Paul was briefly stationed in Heidelberg, a two-hour car journey from Bedfordview, Johannesburg, where we were living at that time. I was so delighted that I would be seeing Paul when I had previously thought it would be about 6 months before I would see him again.

I woke up on that Saturday morning as the sun was tinting the skies with a beautiful amber light. The soft peachy hue that was slowly creeping through a gap in the curtains of my bedroom. I don't know why but my bed always becomes the most comfortable when it is time to awaken. My sheets wrapped around me were comforting and warm, but the anticipation of seeing Paul that morning drove me from the comfort and I started to ready myself for the day. The children were both fast asleep which gave me time to bathe and get ready for the journey. I prepared their bottles for the car and ensured bags were packed with diapers and all the necessities for little ones. When the children awoke I readied them for the journey and before long we were safely ensconced in the car, the babies in their car seats with bottles in hand to quench their thirst.

It was a beautiful day made more glorious with the thought of seeing Paul again. Sunlight filtered through the trees and spread dappled shade on the grass. Eventually after half an hour into the journey the sun shone in all its triumphant beauty promising a rain free, blue sky day. We drove on for 2 hours. Anna, who was only 2 years old didn't fully comprehend what the day was all about but understood enough to know that she would be seeing her daddy. Jay, only 6 months, was cooing at the back of the car, enjoying the ride with absolutely no idea what the day held for us.

It was rather odd that Paul had phoned me late on the Friday evening to inform me that all the men were told that there could be no outward displays of affection, and that he was to salute me when he saw me. I thought that was weird and I protested. However, the military have their protocol and he would have to salute me if he wanted his family to visit him. I didn't want a salute I wanted a hug. However, as I sit here and write this, I think I would rather revel in the salute now. In fact, I would insist on it!

We got to Heidelberg in good time. I am not sure if I obeyed the speed limit the entire journey because I just wanted, and really needed, to see Paul. Separation has always been difficult for us and it never gets easier. When I chide my brother, Geoff, for breaking the speed limit, his cheeky retort is; "Carol, my heart is doing the speed limit but my foot will not co-operate!"

We got out the car and I strapped Jay to my belly with a body sling that we used all those years ago. I took Anna out the car seat and we walked slowly to the parade grounds with Anna clutching my hand. It was an official event because all the high-powered officers were present. There were Generals, Colonels, Captains, Lieutenants and an array of lower ranking officers. It was impressive. I was walking to go and meet Paul when all of a sudden Anna spotted her daddy in the crowd. She let go of my hand immediately and began running. I could not keep up with those swift little legs as she made her way towards him with her blonde hair like golden wheat dancing in the wind. She kept running, oblivious to the fact that there were high ranking military officers. She didn't care because she had seen her daddy. She kept running and when she reached her daddy she literally threw herself into his arms in total abandonment. It was such a beautiful sight that all the high-ranking officials were silent and appreciated the sight of a precious child being re-united with her Dad.

Whenever I have gone through challenging situations I recall that special moment that will live with me until the day I die. Anna had not seen her Dad for some time but she knew him and trusted him. In those times of despair, I see that picture and I abandon myself to the arms of my loving heavenly Father. I throw myself upon Him and know I can trust Him completely.

Every place we have been to and every experience we have had has always taught me valuable lessons. Fiji showed us that God cared about the details of our lives and sent angels to help us. It also revealed an important lesson; always be grateful for every provision God makes, even if it didn't meet our expectations. Fiji showed me that serving God was an adventure and that He would always look after us. And He has. *Radical obedience* is really the only life to live because when you are obedient your life is filled with abundant blessings.

Prayerful Pause:

We are all unique individuals. As the Psalmist proclaimed: We are *fearfully and wonderfully* made. It is also true that we are all different. In chapter eleven of the book of Hebrews, we are encouraged to run the race that God has marked out for us. I love the fact that God has mapped out my race and yours too. Our races may look quite different but I believe that God gives each of us grace to run our individual race. You may look at my journey and think; "What an incredibly wonderful path God has set her on." However, no one knows the challenges and heartaches and difficulties of my race, as I have no real idea of yours. All I do know, is that if as the writer of Hebrews says, we keep our focus on Jesus, He will be with us through every situation, every challenge and difficulty, as well as all the joyful experiences. So, my challenge as you pause here is to reflect on your journey. If you are facing a challenge ask God to give you the strength to keep going. Keep your eyes on Jesus. When you get your focus off the goal you get distracted. Keep your gaze ahead and allow God's grace to uphold you in every season.

Chapter Nine

OBEDIENCE AND THE IMPORTANCE OF TIMING

· · · · · · · · · ·

God uses men [and women] who are
feeble enough to lean on Him

HUDSON TAYLOR

PAUL

After an amazing time in the Pacific Ocean Islands, we arrived in beautiful New Zealand. Our first stop was in Auckland. In ways that we never fully understood, the Assemblies of God churches there had invited us to serve across the nation for about three months. We felt more welcomed than ever before and a delegation was there to meet us off the plane.

We were soon safely accommodated with a wonderful young couple called Ray and Helen Connell. The first meal Helen prepared for us was roast leg of lamb. After months of meals dominated by taro root this was a feast. It was a foretaste of the delightful three months ahead of us.

As mentioned earlier, Carol had perfected the art of ventriloquism. This part of her life is yet another reason why I love her so much and am thankful that we have served together over the years. While still in Pennsylvania at the very early part of our world adventure Carol had come across a ventriloquism course taught through several manuals. Despite the cost we agreed that she should add this skill to her ministry.

The course arrived as did the new ventriloquial dummy. We proceeded to name him Montgomery, for no particular reason at all. He became an integral part of our lives for the following years. I would hear Carol practicing for hours on end. She developed the ability to replace consonants with alternate sounds, project her voice through her nasal passages and very soon became a proficient and talented ventriloquist.

She wrote the script for several Bible lessons. One was about Jonah. When Carol asked Montgomery what the main lesson was from Jonah's story, his retort was that you could not keep a good man down. Soon she was in great demand and by the time we arrived in New Zealand we found opportunities every week to speak in school assemblies.

Once the word was out about Carol's talent, Montgomery became a fixture in every church service in which we spoke including some of the larger churches in New Zealand. I acquired an eight-string ukulele and mastered three chords. Montgomery would sing "This little light of mine," with great gusto. As he reached the crescendo the assembly or congregation would erupt in applause. It was a very special time.

We traveled across both the north and the south islands of New Zealand. We met some of the most hospitable and lovely people. I remember a pastoral couple in Palmerston North had a little conference between themselves and then insisted that we should phone Carol's parents in South Africa. International phone calls were extremely expensive but they wanted to care and be kind. Hospitality is a very special gift and we were discovering the joy of staying with kind and generous people. We determined that when the opportunity arose, we would do the same.

As our time in New Zealand began to come to an end the Assembly of God office in Auckland forwarded a letter to us. It had come from a large church in South Yorkshire in England. We were amazed to read an invitation to become associate pastors of the Rotherham Assembly. It was by the standards of the day a very large church and at the time, the largest Assembly of God church in Great Britain. We were amazed and awed and it did not take us long to respond to the invitation positively.

In the meantime, some correspondence indicated that we would be welcome to visit Australia. This turned into several open doors that would take us to Sydney, Katoomba, where the Commonwealth Bible College was, and then via Melbourne and Adelaide, to Perth, and Western Australia.

We had a fair idea of what our itinerary would look like and wanted to get the bulk of the long-haul flights booked. Again, we had received multiple small gifts and honoraria and saved meticulously. We were finishing our three-month trip in a town just outside of Wellington, New Zealand's capital city.

We located a travel agent and had managed to find out the cost of these air tickets. I counted our stockpile of cash again and again and each time we were exactly $40 New Zealand short of what was required. With just a few days to go I was not too anxious knowing how God had provided for us again and again in previous months. The last possible day for us to purchase the tickets arrived and we still had not received any of the required shortfall.

In another act of *radical obedience,* we walked the short distance to the travel agent and told him of our needs. He checked out the itinerary, gasped a little and told us he needed at least until noon to make the required bookings. We assured him that this was not a problem and left the agency relieved that we still had some hours to find the required forty dollars.

We checked everywhere we could. We unpacked our suitcases, turned out every pocket and looked in all our shoes. The money was nowhere to be found. We duly returned to the agency around noon. The agent was most apologetic and asked if we would be kind enough to allow him the afternoon to finish his work. Again, we were relieved at the reprieve and assured him that this was not an inconvenience to us at all. It certainly felt like a faith journey, and we were sure that we had now been fully tested and found to be true.

As the afternoon drew to a close, we could not understand why God had not provided and this time returned to the travel agency with a feeling of trepidation. The agent was waiting for us, welcomed us into his shop and locked the door behind us. He said that he did not want any disturbances, but I felt trapped and had a sense of a growing embarrassment because we lacked the funds to purchase the tickets that by now had been produced and were lying clearly on the desk before us. All those years ago the shortfall was a significant percentage of the whole and now loomed before us as an embarrassingly large amount.

We checked over the tickets carefully. They were all correct and in order. The agent then began to explain the breakdown of costs and sure enough, we remained short of what was required. I remember reaching for the envelope that had been stuffed in a pocket and began to count out the money. I was thinking seriously about the multiplication of the loaves and fishes and was wondering how God would multiply this wad of cash.

As I neared the end of counting out the notes the agent interrupted me with a strange question. He confirmed that we had flown into the country three months prior. We confirmed this and he went on to ask if we had retained the stubs of the tickets that had brought us to New Zealand. I had a brown zip up travel case in which I kept everything. These were heady days and everything had a story and was worth keeping. I had those stubs carefully stored in my little travel bag.

I handed the agent the two stubs and watched with fascination as he stapled one and then the other on top of the thick collection of air tickets that had taken him all day to produce. With a smile, he pushed them back across the desk at me. My look was obviously a quizzical one and so he explained without me having to ask. With a little smugness on his part, he let us know that now the ticket showed an origin other than somewhere in New Zealand and we would not have to pay departure tax. He then confidently let us know that this amounted to $20 per ticket! It was exactly the shortfall about which we had worried throughout the day. We left that agency with a song in our hearts and the memory of this remarkable provision influenced many decisions throughout the coming decades.

So, we crossed the Tasman Sea and arrived at Sydney. We quickly established the same ministry routine. A church accommodated us in a small apartment and we busily served for several weeks. We received an invitation to travel up the Blue Mountains to minister at Commonwealth Bible College that had recently relocated from Brisbane and moved into a large former hotel in the beautiful mountain town of Katoomba. We met the Principal, a Welshman by the name of Aaron Morgan as well as his lovely wife Dinah. They became dear friends for many years to come.

We ministered briefly in Melbourne before flying on to Adelaide, the capital city of South Australia. We had the privilege of preaching in several churches, including a church in the suburb of Klemzig, that was soon to explode into one of the largest churches in Australia under the outstanding leadership of Andrew Evans. It was a special time in every way, except Carol seemed to be a bit off color each morning.

We flew onto Perth where we were met on the tarmac of the small airport at the time by the leaders of the Assembly of God churches in Western Australia. They had a busy schedule planned for us that included traveling way up north and inland as well.

Before we left we wanted to know why Carol was so ill each day. We found a clinic nearby and I waited anxiously sitting on the brick wall while she went inside. Sometime later she emerged to tell me that the test was positive. I had no idea what she was referring to until she explained to her naïve husband that she was pregnant with our first child. We were overcome with joy and trepidation. We had no home, no secure employment, and a lot of travel still ahead of us.

It did not help that the only way to meet all the demands of the itinerary that we had was to fly around in a four-seater plane. For several weeks, the churches made this little plane and a delightful pilot, available to us. We flew several hours north to a town called Karratha. It was so very hot and the only cool air in the room was through louvres that opened in the walls. Within seconds of getting outside, our backs would be covered with flies. It was like nowhere we had ever been before, but we were loving every minute—except for the morning sickness.

After a week of serving in the school, youth services and multiple church services we left in the small plane for a fascinating place called Mount Tom Price. A few years before a prospector had been flying over the barren expanse of Western Australia when a sudden rain shower dampened the ground beneath his plane. To his amazement the earth changed color and reflected an eerie light back at him. He quickly marked his location and later found his way overland to that exact place. His hunch was correct, and he discovered possibly the largest iron ore deposit in the world. The ore was so dense that it was possible to ark-weld the rocks together.

A small interdenominational group of Christians had begun to gather in this extremely remote location, and we had the joy of conducting Bible studies and services with them for the next week or so. Then it was back to Geraldton, and finally to Perth. Over the coming years we had the joy of returning to some of these places as well as serving churches in the southwest of the state.

Lessons were being learnt, our little girl was on her way and our amazing time in New Zealand and Australia was coming to an end. We were England bound but not before another brief adventure.

We took advantage of an almost free addition to our flights to return to South Africa and briefly see our parents. Whether it was the sense of home, the security of being with family or something else, we both encountered a deep weariness. We had traveled thousands of miles, slept on dozens and dozens of beds and conducted on average about twelve services a week for months. We both found ourselves sleeping for long hours. In retrospect, we were spiritually, emotionally, and physically exhausted.

How I wish that someone could have had the insight to discern this. But neither we nor anyone else really understood the emotional state that we were in. It would take several more such experiences before we began to recognize the early signs of exhaustion and take precautionary action.

Carol's younger brother Geoff joined us as we traveled on to Israel. We found a guest house just outside the ancient walls of Jerusalem. Soon we were connected to an elderly British missionary who took us under his wings. We preached to the small group of Christ followers that he had gathered. We were there only about ten years after the six-day war and much of East Jerusalem was still in ruins. It was a fascinating experience spending time with someone who was so deeply invested in the ancient city and its people. I remember one day gazing over the ruins when our friend reminded us that, despite the dismal view, it was in this place that God had chosen to make His name known.

We traveled on to Athens. A church opened its doors and provided accommodation. Geoff was awed to see how God provided. We realized that we had become accustomed to God's kind and providential care of us. For Geoff, it was almost a daily amazement. It was in Athens that Carol's puppet Montgomery spoke to hundreds of children through an interpreter. It was very humorous to see the interpreter speak to the puppet as if he was a real person and ask him to repeat what he had just said. The Greek kids roared with laughter and the Gospel was proclaimed.

Then it was on to England where an entirely different experience awaited us. It would need just as much *radical obedience* as the nearly two years of global travel and ministry had required.

Prayerful pause:

Although this chapter might have provoked several responses as you read it, let me challenge you in two areas. Firstly, the tension that often exists between time and eternity can cause distress and uncertainty. We faced this for a whole day while waiting to see God's provision for our air tickets. At times the process of waiting for God's provision or answer to prayer can be agonizing. Pray now for the grace, faith and patience to see your season through. May you receive God's reassurance that he knows what is going on and will provide in His way and in His time. Secondly, recall with me our experience as we gazed over the ruins of Jerusalem. From ancient times God said he would put His name there. Because of the saving work of Jesus, God now puts His name in our hearts. This never changes. Perhaps you are looking at the ruins of a dream, the challenges of a broken relationship or some other sadness or negative setback. Prayerfully remind yourself that God's name is written on your heart, and He will not leave or forsake you.

Chapter Ten

HARD OBEDIENCE

· · · · · · · · · ·

There are two things to do about the
gospel. Believe it and behave it.
Susanna Wesley

CAROL

If we believe the Bible, and we embody those beliefs, it will impact the way we behave. The only possible way to respond rightly to the Bible, is by living out loud what we believe. In other words, *radical obedience* is not optional. After all our adventures, we were on our way to England to take up the role of Associate Pastor in an influential and large church in Rotherham, South Yorkshire. We were excited and apprehensive all at once. Little did we know what awaited us. I often think that it is a good thing that we cannot always glimpse down the corridor of time. If we went into all the rooms that make up the different experiences of our lives, we might never have ventured down that particular passage.

Before going to England, some wonderful friends, who we had got to know while we were in Bible College, invited us to Cairnbulg, Scotland. Cairnbulg, is a beautiful little fishing village in the North East of Scotland. We arrived in time for 'Hogmanay,' which is the Scottish word for New Year's Eve, and it is associated with wonderful festivities. The Scots are a wonderful and generous people, despite the unfair wrap they get for being labeled frugal. They are a hearty people and they know how to celebrate. Hogmanay affords them the opportunity to have fun and to have a party. The tradition also includes 'first-footing' where you enter people's homes after midnight, and take gifts like shortbread and other sweet goodies and you eat together, celebrating the beginning of another year.

My younger brother Geoff, who was only fifteen years old at the time was traveling with us during his Christmas vacation. We stayed with our friends and another wonderful couple hosted my brother. You need to understand that the Scottish brogue up in the North East is broad and at times it can sound like a foreign language. Geoff, who had never been to the North East before had particular trouble understanding the couple with whom he stayed. When they spoke to him he had to keep saying; "Pardon, could you repeat that?" However, after you have asked someone to repeat something three times it becomes quite embarrassing. At that point Geoff would just answer in the affirmative. This caused some embarrassment when we discovered that he had confessed to having a girlfriend, who was the love of his life, and who he was definitely going to marry. He had no idea he was saying yes to these questions, when actually he had up to that point never had a girlfriend. We have had many laughs over the years about that time in Scotland.

After our New Year celebrations, we headed to Rotherham, in England to one of the largest Assembly of God churches at that time. We were going to take up our new role in the church. It was pastored at that time by the senior pastor, who had been the President at the Bible College some years before.

To our horror we discovered that the house which had been promised to us was only the back room of the house in which he was living. I was a young wife and expecting our first baby and so living with a single man, who had lived many years separated from his wife, was a challenge indeed. I will spare the reader the details, but to say it was a trying time for both of us would be the understatement of the year.

Paul quickly realized that if we were both to preserve our sanity we would need to get a little home of our own. We had a small amount of money saved but we had bucket loads of determination to get out of the house in which we were living. We found a small house and decided that we wanted to purchase it, but we had no idea as to how we would be able to get a mortgage. Fortunately, a member of our church heard of our predicament and offered us his help. He was a successful insurance agent, and had good contacts with the Halifax Building Society. With no earnings record or credit check we were amazed when he called us to say that he had called in a favor, and that we would be able to finance our home. This all happened in a short space of time and we were able to move into our own little home before our first baby entered the world. Furnishing our home was another huge miracle. People in the church helped us with beds and furniture for our baby and a whole array of other necessities. We saw the kind hand of our loving God meeting us in such practical ways.

My beautiful mother, Audrey, flew all the way from Port Shepstone, Natal, in South Africa to be there for the birth of our first baby. My Dad, brother Geoff, and younger sister Tracy, would follow a month later. It was so wonderful to have my mom with us. We went for beautiful walks in the English countryside. The intoxicating fragrances of early summer, with daffodils carpeting the ground in a golden glow, warmed our hearts and filled us with expectation for the birth of our first child.

My mom had been with us for a month and there was still no sign of our first born. One day before the rest of the family arrived, the doctor told me to pack to my bags and head to Netheredge Hospital, Sheffield. I entered my ward on the twenty first of June 1978, to be induced. In the early hours of the morning, when the sky was still pitch black, I felt the first pangs of labor. I lay in bed as the pains came in waves and then went as swiftly. I could hardly wait to meet our baby.

As sunlight tinted the skies with rusty hues and warmth filtered through the hospital windows, I was wheeled to the room in which I would birth my baby. On the twenty second of June 1978, at 12.10pm our baby girl, Anna Carol, entered the world and changed our lives. She had strawberry blonde hair, green eyes and was the most perfect sight we had ever laid our eyes on. It was if our eyes were hungry because we just could not get enough of the magnificent gift God had brought into our lives. When your babies enter the world, your lives are forever changed. You experience a love so deep that it is difficult to verbalize.

My family were besotted with Anna, and there was no lack of affection or attention poured out on our little girl. They stayed with us for a whole month and we reveled in every moment we had with them. Paul and I had left home when we were just seventeen and eighteen years old. Time with my family has always been special and I have wonderful memories tucked away in my mind, and when they resurface I am always filled with gratitude for my family.

Two days after Anna was born Paul and I went to our church prayer meeting. I was able to leave Anna with my parents even though she was only a couple of days old. When the prayer meeting ended, the senior pastor asked if he could meet with me and Paul in his office. We walked in and were surprised to see two other church officers in the room. He told us to take our seats. There was almost an audible silence. The senior pastor spoke into the room shattering the stillness as he looked directly at me. Each word had a staccato like precision as I sat there mute and paralyzed listening to what he was saying. "You are a selfish girl," he quipped. I sat waiting as each word hit me with a death like blow. "You expect your husband to visit you and your baby in hospital when people in the church need him." He continued unabated, "It is evident you do not love people." On and on he went, his words hitting like a hammer beating out any remnant of self-esteem I might have had. I felt utterly broken. I was twenty years old; I had sought to serve God in obedience and now I was being told in no uncertain terms that I did not begin to measure up to his expectations or in his view, God's expectations of me. I felt despair cling to me like a grey cloud diffusing all over me, leaving my mouth dry and my vocal cords frozen. I got up from my seat, accompanied by Paul, and tears flowed in unrelenting torrents down my cheeks.

As we walked out the meeting, a wonderful man, who would become a great friend and ally, saw the tears and immediately determined to follow us up. Gordon and Vera Pepper became like parents to us. I would never have survived that year in Rotherham without the love and care these wonderful friends poured out on us during our time there.

I do not know why the senior pastor sought to be so unkind. I should add that we were not the only recipients of his unkindness. What I do know is that Paul and I determined once again from that day on that we would never treat young people with disrespect or unkindness. We would always endeavor to love and encourage them and if we needed to speak the truth, we would always seek to do it in a caring and compassionate way. That decision has been one of the foundations of our ministry. If I had not undergone such unkind treatment, perhaps we would never have learned this valuable lesson.

A few months later, Paul was conscripted into the South African military and received his instructions to report for duty. This meant that we would be leaving England and if the truth be told, I was so thankful to be out of the toxic leadership environment into which we had been introduced. I do not say all of this to be critical but simply to let the reader know that life is not always fair and that even the best of leaders have feet of clay. There were many wonderful people in that large church and they were kind and generous to us throughout our stay, but their care and concern was always overshadowed by the harsh way in which we were treated by the leadership of that church.

Some weeks after receiving the conscription paper we received another letter saying that Paul's military service had been delayed for a year. This was a blow, as even separation and serving in the military was a better option than our current toxic situation.

A few days later, we were surprised by a phone call from Pastor Sam Ennis, who led a large church on the west side of Johannesburg. With no formalities, he warmly invited us to join him on the pastoral team with a particular commitment to the youth. We said we would pray earnestly and give him an answer. It did not take us long to make the decision to serve alongside Sam and Louise Ennis. Those were wonderful days of friendship and deep healing for our souls.

By early December 1978, Anna was six months old, our friends Gordon and Vera Pepper, along with other good friends from Rotherham, drove us to Heathrow airport to catch a plane back to our city of birth, Johannesburg. The thought of Paul serving in the military felt a bit overwhelming but we were both excited to see our parents and siblings once again. We arrived back on a beautiful December day.

As we stepped outside the plane, we felt the warmth of the sun and it seemed as if everything was right in the world. We were home! Paul's parents were at the airport to meet us and to welcome their first granddaughter home. I can still see it all, with the picture emblazoned clearly in my mind; there was the joy, the relief and great hope filling my expectations for what lay ahead.

We started our time with Sam Ennis in Roodepoort. Sam was an unthreatened leader with a beautiful heart. The church board rented a little home and we lived there for the first few months. It was not in a great neighborhood and so Paul and I began discussing buying a house so that Anna and I would be safe when Paul was in the military in a year's time.

We soon found out that we would be bringing another baby into the world and so our lives were filled with ministry, family responsibilities, entertaining guests, and with joy and deep contentment.

A wonderful church elder, I cannot remember his name, because everyone called him "brother Robbie," helped us to buy a house. We found a lovely three bedroomed home with a swimming pool and lots of fruit trees in Florida Glen. When I saw the house, my eyes lit up as if the blinds had just been opened. It was a good neighborhood with tree lined streets, paved walkways and nice houses. The only problem was that the house was being auctioned when we were away visiting my parents in Port Shepstone, Natal. Brother Robbie went to the auction and being a brilliant negotiator we had full confidence that he would get the house at the asking price of forty-six thousand rand. At that time, that would have been about twenty-two thousand dollars.

The first mortgage holder came to the auction; however, the second mortgage holder did not bother attending. Brother Robbie was able to get us our home for twenty-four thousand rand. We were utterly ecstatic. With a new little one arriving in January, and Paul going into the military, it was an answer to prayer. Paul, was given the opportunity to serve as one of three, who were the first Pentecostal Chaplains, in the South African military. That alone was a wonderful answer to prayer as Paul felt God had opened a wonderful door for ministry during his service. God is so good and faithful.

Paul was due to leave for the military on the 12th January 1980. On the 9th of January, the baby was still resting contented in my womb. I was anxious as I did want Paul to be present for the birth of our second child. The morning of 10th January, God heard our anxious cries. At 4.00am I woke Paul and told him we were having our baby. I took a long bath and we left for the hospital at 6.00am. At 8.20am our precious son, Jason Paul came screaming into the world. Again, he changed our lives forever. Anna, was so delighted to have a baby brother and she nurtured him and fussed over him like a caring little sister does.

Paul will tell the story of serving in the military in the next chapter. When Paul left on the 12th of January, I felt overwhelmed. I confess I cried relentlessly as I waved him goodbye at our dining room window. Pastor Same Ennis was taking him to the army headquarters in Pretoria; from there he was sent to basic training at an elite unit in a town called Heidelberg. You will recall that I shared a story about a visit to Paul some six months later in Heidelberg.

The church at Roodepoort were so kind and caring to me when Paul left. During the entire time of Paul's military stint, they looked after us financially. We are forever grateful for our time with Pastor Sam and Louise Ennis. Sam is in heaven, and I know he heard: "Well done, good and faithful servant." Sometimes *radical obedience* presents us with challenges, but I would not choose a different life. It has been worth it all.

Prayerful Pause:

I know this period for me was a lonely and anxious time. However, in the midst of it all I was more conscious than ever of God's goodness and faithfulness. If you are experiencing a unique situation and feel you cannot go another day, let me assure you that I have been there on numerous occasions. We are humans, with complicated emotions and we sometimes feel more strongly than we ever thought we could. I urge you to pause right now and pray that God will give you the strength to see through this season. The psalmist said that weeping endures for the night and then joy comes in the morning. Let me assure you that the darker the night, the more joy there is when morning does come. Keep courage my friend, God will see you through. Trust Him.

Chapter Eleven

OBEDIENCE IN
UNIFORM

· · · · · · · · · · ·

*Obedience is an expression of love and the acting out of
mutual responsibility, we place others before ourselves*

St Benedict of Nursia

PAUL

A part of our lives that we have seldom shared is the very challenging time
that we faced due to my conscription to the South African army. South
Africa was a sparsely populated part of the African continent for most of
its history. Over centuries tribes had slowly moved south and occupied
land. At the southern tip of the continent a group of people closely related
to the San Bushmen were the predominant inhabitants. These were the
Hottentots of Southern Africa.

By the late 1400's a Portuguese explorer by the name of Bartholomew
Dias, had navigated around the Cape of Good Hope and planted several
crosses up the east coast of Africa. It was not until almost two centuries
later that trade routes began to open, and the Dutch East India Company
was dominating global business.

For Southern Africa, everything was about to change. A victualling
station was established in what is today Cape Town and a governor was
appointed. As in all European settlements, there was conflict with the local

inhabitants. Eventually, because of disease, conflict and intermarriage, the Hottentots disappeared as a distinct people group. Others quickly took their place.

Napoleon began his rampage across Europe, culminating in his disastrous march on Moscow in 1812. Prior to this, he invaded the Netherlands and, fearing he would potentially control the lucrative trade around the Cape of Good Hope, the Dutch asked for British protection for their small colony. The British assumed this responsibility with relish and soon established rule over the colony in the name of the Crown.

Most of the population by this time were Dutch settlers. Many of these settlers were Huguenots who had fled from various regions of France during the counter Reformation. Their Protestant Dutch friends, received them but encouraged many to seek free citizenship by migrating to the colony in Southern Africa.

They soon had prosperous farms and vineyards but had a tense relationship with their British overlords. Eventually, these hardy famers decided they could no longer live in a British colony and in 1835 they came together and began what was to be known as: The Great Trek. Hundreds of deeply devout people, who shared a commitment to the reformed tradition of Christian faith, put their trust in their God and with determination headed north.

From the outset, these pious people believed that their future and their land was in the hands of their God. They adopted the Exodus narrative from the Bible as their own and soon saw many parallels between their journey into the African hinterland and that of the Israelites being led by the great law-giver-Moses. These brave pioneers became known as the Voortrekkers.

This close association with the biblical narrative would prove to be very problematic to successive generations. Amongst the multiple stories that would enter Afrikaner (as these people became known) legend, one in particular stood out. After crossing the spine of mountains that runs down the eastern side of southern Africa, the Voortrekkers encountered the mighty Zulu kingdom, led by the great chief-Dingaan. There were some minor diplomatic efforts made to try to coexist, but these failed and ended in bloodshed. The battle lines were drawn. Thousands of Zulu "impis" (warriors) descended on just a few hundred Voortrekkers who had drawn their wagons together into a laager.

It was December 16th, 1838, when the new settlers defended their small encampment. They made a vow that if God would deliver them, they would forever remember and honor this day. Women and children loaded the guns and men furiously fired them. Wave upon wave of Zulu warriors fell as they ran into the firing, many with the belief that their witchdoctors had given them potions to prevent the bullets from harming them. In the end, the Voortrekkers suffered three wounded compared to the tragic loss of between twenty-five thousand and thirty thousand Zulus.

This single day, which became known as the Day of the Vow, was sadly a harbinger of the next one hundred and fifty years of South Africa's sad history. It was into this tragic racial conflict that I was born and now faced the dilemma of wearing the uniform of a white nationalist army.

We had often been conflicted about returning to South Africa, after graduating from Bible college. In 1979 the first ever commission for Pentecostal Chaplains was established and in ways that I have never truly understood, I was nominated as one of four who could serve in this capacity. The non-combatant nature of this call-up helped us make the decision to return to South Africa from England.

Two days after our son Jason was born, I said a sad farewell to my little family, leaving Carol with two children under eighteen months of age and made my way to report for duty. I remember glancing back and seeing Carol with tears in her eyes holding Anna in her arms and waving through the dining room window. It was the hardest farewell I had ever endured.

Soon we were being shouted at by corporals several years our junior as about a hundred of us chaplains from various denominational backgrounds went through basic training. It was as demanding as any infantry soldier. We were based with an elite unit and the army was determined to put us through the same rigors as everyone else.

Food was roughly slopped onto metal plates; daily drills took place on the parade ground and we were subjected to long night marches in damp and freezing weather. I was determined to live out my faith in this environment, just as I had in the previous years of ministry. I remember asking the sergeant if any provision was made for us as ministers to have a daily devotion. With most days starting at 5.00 am it seemed as though there would not be time for devotions. After much discussion, it was agreed that we would not be required to be on duty before 5.30 am each day.

This arrangement worked well for about two weeks. One morning there was great commotion, and we were being rushed to assemble on the parade ground very soon after 5.00 am. I am not sure how wise it was, but I refused to fall in line. I stood apart from the group and complained. It was not well received. I knew by then that if I was to pay for my insolence I might as well hold out as long as I could. I felt obviously nervous as I was shouted at first by the corporals and then a very irate sergeant and finally by all my compatriots.

I do not know how I had the nerve to hold my ground but I did. It was very intimidating but trying to keep my voice steady, I reminded the sergeant that he had told me that we could always make an appeal and so I asked that the lieutenant should be called. The atmosphere grew even more tense when the lieutenant stormed out of the building and standing only a few hands breadths away threatened me with severe consequences. I reminded him that while we were all aware of the need for basic training, we were also chaplains and had been promised time for our spiritual lives. Realizing that this lieutenant was not going to help I asked that the captain be called.

We never saw the captain. A few minutes later a red-faced corporal dismissed us to our rooms for thirty minutes. My fellow chaplains complained bitterly to me that we would pay for my insolence for the rest of the day. Thirty minutes later we lined up on the parade ground again and the day proceeded without any significant difference to every other day. For the remainder of basic training, we were never required to report before 5.30 am again.

Soon basic training was over. I only saw Carol and the children a few times during this time. The separation was terrible. I was then posted to the Army Headquarters in Pretoria to undergo officer's training. A month later our commissioning parade was planned.

Carol and the children traveled to Pretoria as I was commissioned as a full lieutenant. I was given a few days leave before my next posting. It was sheer bliss to be at home for those few days.

I was posted to serve a light aircraft squadron, situated about two hours' drive from home. As an officer, I had a little more freedom and so commuted on occasion. I found myself accompanying pilots, in these small but fast planes, almost every day. Multiple opportunities to serve God presented themselves. I was able to pray at parades, serve different groups of soldiers and be available to dozens of needy young men.

After only two months of relative routine and being able to be with the family quite regularly, the season I dreaded came. For years the political situation in Southern Africa had deteriorated. Fueled by the ambitions of the Eastern Block, led by communist Russia and Eastern Germany, the region was a tinder box. The Rhodesian civil war had ended in December 1979 with a disastrous accord called the Lancaster House Agreement. The two Portuguese colonies of Mozambique and Angola were rapidly descending into civil war. Zambia wanted to insert itself into the conflict and the only thing holding all of these nations together was their combined determination to end white rule in South Africa. They became known as the "Front Line" states.

The South African regime was determined to hold onto power and moved resources and troops to its northern borders. One of these borders was on the northern edge of the South African protectorate called South West Africa, now Namibia. The border was broken into sectors and I was posted to serve in sector One Zero. It was at the center of a low intensity war that involved patrolling on foot, gathering intelligence and making contact with the mobile forces of the South West African Peoples Organization (SWAPO). Unfortunately, the local population were often caught in the middle of this conflict.

The Headquarters for the sector were in a place called Ondangwa. This was also where the air force base was located. I left home, climbed into a Hercules 160 aircraft and flew, strapped into webbing in the dark belly of the plane for four hours towards the northwest. As a precaution against Sam 7 missiles, the planes would come in at high altitude and then rapidly corkscrew downwards often resulting in heavy landings. This was exactly my welcome. I was assigned to Charlie Company which was based on the Angolan border, outside a little town called Okankolo.

Two incidents are worth recording. The first demonstrated my deep conviction that God works constantly in our lives. The area had seen a lot of action. I had assisted in an operation following a terrible landmine incident involving a pick-up truck packed with about fifteen local people.

They drove over the mine, detonated it and only three survived. It was left to our doctor and me to retrieve the shredded body parts and place them in body bags. We called in a helicopter and were able to rush the three survivors to hospital.

We knew the dangers facing us each time we left the base. On one occasion, we were required to attend a commanding officer's conference in Ondangwa. I had the most senior rank and so was required to be convoy commander. I ordered the drivers to cut the engines on our armored vehicles, removed my bush hat and asked all the men in the three vehicles to stand and allow me to pray. With a few grumbles, they did so. As I said amen a corporal came bounding out of the communications tent to say that we did not need to drive and that they were sending small plane to collect me and our commanding officer. We were all relieved. We had a small landing strip adjacent to the camp.

No sooner had we disembarked when another signal came through saying the plane was not coming. We mounted the vehicles and as we reached the gate were informed of another possible plane. I knew the airstrip needed the engineers to sweep for landmines. So, we parked the vehicles and I sent the troops to the mess to get some food.

Soon I heard a groan coming from the mess and found out that the plane was not coming after all. I asked the engineers to sweep the road instead of the airstrip so as to give us a head start on a safe surface. I distinctly felt that I should tell them to sweep the side of the road which they did, even though they considered it counterintuitive.

We finished our brunch, climbed into the vehicles again and once again I had them cut the engines and stand as I prayed. I asked for God's protection and as I said amen there was a huge blast from about half a mile down the road leading from the camp. Hurried radio exchanges followed and I saw the faces of the radio operators light up with amazement and relief.

The engineers had discovered a double landmine planted the night before. One was planted on top of the other and connected with a cortzite fuse. Remarkably, they discovered it on the side of the road. We often drove there to be safe as the obvious place for landmines was on the track in the road where most vehicles would travel. It was too entrenched to safely defuse it and so the engineers had blown it up. It was meant for us and if the events of the morning had not gone the way they did we would certainly have detonated it. Immediately many of the young men declared that they always wanted to ride in my vehicle from that time forward. The care of a loving God was obvious to us all.

A young lieutenant approached me one day asking that I support his application for compassionate leave. He had been assured that he could leave after several weeks of service, to attend his brother's wedding. I went through all the normal welfare channels but to no avail. I was frustrated and he was desperate. It seemed as though no one was willing to help fulfil the assurance he had been given.

I negotiated with our company commanding officer and he agreed to allow me to travel with the young man to the headquarters and try to work things out. As we made the long and uncomfortable journey it reminded me of a previous frustration I had with army welfare. A young soldier was beside himself worrying about his pregnant wife. He was certain that the baby should have been born but we had no contact from his home unit. I eventually accompanied him to the HQ and arranged for a reverse charge phone call. We were very remote, and these calls were hard to arrange. The sergeant setting up the call asked for the soldier's name. When I told him, he began opening printed communiques that had been thrown into the garbage. He never found the document but nonchalantly informed the young soldier that he recalled receiving the message that his wife had given birth. I was incensed and informed the sergeant that he should put the call through at his expense and allow the young soldier to talk to his wife for as long as he wanted. The sergeant complied knowing that if I escalated the issue, he would most likely lose his rank.

Now I was on my way again and wondered what new inefficiencies I would find. To my surprise my rank was sufficient, and it was not long before I had arranged a flight back to Pretoria for the young man to attend his brother's wedding. I made the tedious journey in the armored vehicle back to base, thinking that was the end of the matter.

From time to time, I joined the small units of soldiers on foot patrol. It was hot and the terrain was difficult. I had always decided that I would not carry a weapon, but I was prepared to carry extra water and radio equipment. The boys seemed happy to have me along. We never knew if or when we would walk into an ambush and we had lost several good young men in these engagements. On the second day, we found a shady tree and threw an antenna into the branches to gain radio contact with the base.

To my surprise the commanding officer was on the radio and asked to speak to me. He was laughing his head off. He told me that I was in serious trouble and was on orders to appear before the sector commander as soon as possible. He was laughing because it was the first time he had ever heard of a chaplain being in this kind of trouble. I had no idea what I had done wrong.

Again, I made the two-hour bone rattling journey to HQ and was marched into the colonel's office. He was fuming. He went to great length to tell me (while sitting in an air-conditioned office) that he was fighting a war and how dare I take one of his officers away from the front and send him back to Pretoria. It took me a while to understand what he was getting at. He threatened me, told me that I had overstepped my rank, and he was considering referring this to higher authorities.

I was never really a good military man and did not feel very intimidated by his bluff and bluster. Then I remembered my issue with the young man who was a danger to himself and his fellow soldiers because of the failure of the communications office to inform him of the birth of his child. I informed the colonel that I, too was fighting his war. In fact, I was seeing far more of the war including dead bodies and destructive landmines than he had ever seen. I explained that just the previous night our base had come under attack with several mortars destroying a part of it. I then went on to tell him of how I had to deal with the inefficiencies of his HQ and that it was no wonder that I took some things into my own hands. I remember thinking that I was probably on my way to a court martial!

As I spoke the colonel became strangely quiet. When I finished, he reached across the desk, shook my hand and invited me to the officer's mess for brunch. The matter was closed.

My years of service were fruitful. Young lives were impacted by the love of God, families whose sons had been killed were comforted and the sacrifice, though hard and at times painful was worth it in terms of God's Kingdom.

Prayerful Pause:

Life often places demands on us for which we did not ask or we would never choose. These circumstances often test *radical obedience*, even more than those faith stretching experiences that are a part of our journey of faith and obedience. This would be a good time for you to pause and reinterpret the things that have been the hardest and even detestable in your life. Perhaps it was a job unfairly lost, a season in which you were badly misrepresented or something else that would be easy to resent and could be the cause of bitterness in your experiences. We are assured that God can turn everything for good if we will allow him to. May He do that for you now.

Chapter Twelve

OBEDIENCE BRINGS DISRUPTION

. . . .

Understanding is the reward of faith. Therefore,
seek not to understand that you may believe,
but believe that you may understand

AUGUSTINE OF HIPPO

CAROL

Our time at Roodepoort saw much fruit. We had incredible growth in our youth group. Paul also took charge of the church when Pastor Sam had a massive heart attack. He recovered and came back, some months later, fully recovered, to lead with vigor and energy. It was a time where I saw Paul's leadership gift grow and his preaching gift was appreciated by all.

Many of the young people in our youth group are serving God in ministry today. Numbers of them came and studied at Africa School of Missions some years later. Paul will tell that story later in this book.

Living as the wife of an army Chaplain was not easy. I was on my own with two little ones under the age of two. These were difficult days in South Africa. There were times I wondered if I would get the dreaded message that Paul had been killed and would be coming home in a body bag. They were tenuous days. It was not uncommon to see military vehicles driving around neighborhoods as Chaplains had to deliver families the sad news of the death of a loved one. I always got the shudders when I saw one of those military vehicles. The visit to a family of a soldier killed in battle, was one of Paul's tasks while serving in the military. It was an aspect of his job that he dreaded.

God was faithful to me during that time as a single mom. We had a German Shepherd dog that one of Paul's Chaplain friends had given us. His name was Pungie. It is a strange name but it was the name we inherited with the dog. So, this good looking, black haired, loving dog, came to live with us.

Pungie was a Godsend. He was the protector of our family when Paul was away. No one, except Paul, was ever allowed to touch me or the children. You could talk to one of us, but you were not allowed to have physical contact. We had a man that mowed our lawn for us in Florida Glen. He quickly learned that he could not make any physical contact with me, Anna or Jay. If I handed Joseph a cup of coffee, Pungie growled and showed his teeth, threatening to attack him if he attempted any contact. We learned a strategy to help deal with the problem. I would place the coffee on the table outside, walk back inside, and then Joseph could proceed to get his coffee. Pungie liked Joseph and never had an issue with him; he was just not allowed to touch or get too close to the three of us. When Anna and Jay were playing in the yard, Pungie followed them around like a hawk, never leaving their sides. That dog was a gift from heaven to us while Paul served in the military. I always felt safe with Pungie there.

As a single mom, with Paul away, I remember the loneliness and sometimes despair that I felt. One day, I was looking out my window, and as I unravel the memory from my mind, I recall that winter was fading, and the first signs of spring were heralding its arrival with splashes of soft pink and mauve colors. I find spring intoxicating as the trees clothe themselves in peachy and white blossoms, bidding the barrenness of winter a joyous farewell. The beauty of the moment didn't diminish the loneliness I felt. In fact, it simply intensified the feeling. I remember crying; "God, I want to serve you, yet all I do is clean the house, cook food, wash diapers, and look after my babies." I heard that still small voice speaking into the depths of my being answering; "You *are* serving me. Caring for your family, nurturing them, and training them in My ways, is serving and honoring me." Then I heard the Lord say; "Enjoy this season because it will soon pass." To be a mom is a wonderful privilege that not everyone is afforded. To those who are blessed with the gift of motherhood and being a stay-at-home mom, let me say that your job is as much a calling as any. I sought from that moment on, to pause, appreciate the season and nurture my family to the best of my ability. I have not always succeeded as I would have wanted but I have tried.

The sadness for me, was that Paul missed so many of the early months of our children's lives and they missed their Dad being an intrinsic part of those years. However, at that time in South Africa, serving in the military was compulsory and so I have to believe that God knew all about it. Circumstances are not always optimal; we do not always understand the why of every situation and season we go through. I do know that God upheld us during that time, and I also know that God used Paul in a special way as he served as a military Chaplain in the armed forces. Obedience is not always easy, and at times there are sacrifices, but I will echo this throughout my life; *radical obedience* is the best and only option for an abundant life.

The day finally arrived when Paul's long stint in the military came to an end. He would have other short periods of service for a number of years, but the long stretch was finally over. The children and I drove the journey to go and fetch Paul for the final time. Jay and Anna were safely ensconced in their car seats at the back. The children were always contented driving, and the hum of the engine often lulled them to sleep. Listening to their rhythmic breathing and knowing they were content always gave me a warm feeling.

We eventually arrived at our destination, and Paul was already waiting anxiously for us. One of the most precious moments for Paul, was when he walked up to the car, and opened the back door to say hello and hug the children. Jay had not seen his daddy for many months, and Paul was quite apprehensive about how he would respond to seeing him again. He wondered if Jay would even recognize him. Jay saw his Dad, and his little blue eyes lit up instantly; a radiant smile spread across his face as he mumbled: "Dada." There are moments in time that are never forgotten, and they live in your heart and mind; this was one of those. Paul's eyes filled with tears of joy and gratitude as he embraced the three of us and thanked God that we were all safe and together again. Separation is difficult and nothing can compensate for the times missed, the moments lost, the opportunities for fathering his children, but we have always chosen to live hope filled lives, to count our blessings, live for the day, and be thankful for each precious day we are given.

When I reflect on this time, it was hard and lonely. However, in every situation I have always sought to look for the positive. The negative is so easy to find. As human beings, we seem to be wired at times to respond negatively. So, you might be reading and thinking what an awful season of life that must have been. I can answer assuredly; God did so much on the inside of me during that time that I cannot allow myself to live with regrets.

We were back living in the comfort of our lovely little home in Florida Glen. We had even built on an addition of a small study and guest room to our home. We settled into a comfortable routine, found our rhythm and enjoyed being a family. We had not even finished furnishing our addition of new rooms when we got a call from one of the Board Members of our home church, Fairview Assembly of God, in Johannesburg. Paul was a mere twenty-four years old and I was coming up to twenty-three. We had lived a lot of life in our short earthly span. The call was to ask Paul if he would be available to serve as senior pastor of our home church. We felt deeply honored and humbled but at the same time apprehensive and unsure. We knew that the church had gone through a difficult season, and that under the previous leader there had been a church split in which more than half the congregation had left the church to follow the former leader. Most of the affluent people who had supported the church financially, left with him.

The church was broken, divided and in many respects dysfunctional. As with every invitation we prayed. Paul agreed to an interview where the entire church Board were present. After that meeting and much prayer, we both felt led to take up the position. We did this in raw obedience, not because it was attractive and certainly not because the money was good. I will add here, that money has never been a motivation for me and Paul. If God has called us to a place of service, then the answer should always be "yes" not "how much?" We have always believed that if God did not meet our need in one way, He would provide through another avenue. We can put our hands on our hearts and say that obedience for us has never ever been decided based on finance. I do not excuse church Boards who are miserly. It is our belief that church Boards should look after their pastor to the best of their ability. However, there are times when churches do not have adequate finances to support a pastor. That should never deter anyone who feels they are called to a particular place. The only thing that should propel us is the call of God. I hold fast to the fact that; as Hudson Taylor, the missionary to China said: "God's work done in God's way will never lack God's supply."

We have ensured that when it comes to any major life change or decision, we both pray and seek God. Paul has always honored and respected me, and we have always ensured that the decision we make is a joint one where both of us find absolute unity and peace. That is the way we have operated all through our lives. If one of us have a check in our spirit, that is enough for us to give serious consideration as to whether we proceed or not.

It is true to say, we also believed that God gave us our children and they are and were an intrinsic part of our present and future. We have never been afraid to lay a calling and ministry before the whole family and ask each one to pray about it. If God calls us, it is as a family. God loves the family, and what is good for one will be good for all. I am not denying that there may be challenging times for a particular member of the family, but I do hold fast to the belief that God is intrinsically involved in the family unit, not just one person's calling. So, whenever there was a family decision to make, our children always knew because we called a family meeting in the lounge. There was always a pot of tea on the tray accompanied by decadent pastries. When the kids saw the pastries, they always knew there was some decision that needed to be made involving our future. Oh, those were always fun times and precious moments. We would take hours sipping tea, talking, answering their questions, and praying, all the while demolishing pastry after pastry with impunity. That was one time I did not count calories and allowed the children to indulge.

Going to Fairview, for me, was like going home. The church bought a three-bedroomed parsonage, with a swimming pool in the same area in which I had grown up. Many South Africans had pools in their backyard for those hot summer days. There was never any air conditioning in the homes and so a pool did feel more like a necessity than a luxury. In fact, it was two blocks from my childhood home.

It was not the same church that Paul and I had left as young people. There was no youth work in the church, Sunday School was sorely diminished, and the people who remained were discouraged. Many of their friends had left in the split and they had remained, not because they wanted to but out of sheer loyalty. Division is costly and never yields good fruit. The split never prospered and eventually that leader left ministry completely.

We began to see expansion in the church as young people began to fill the pews. One evening, after a weekly women's meeting I held, two young men arrived on their motor bike. They were dressed in black, their hair was ruffled from the ride, and in my eyes, they looked terrifying. One of them was a young man named Errol Mustafa. He looked at me with his piercing dark eyes and said; "Don't be scared, we are Christians, we just want to find out when your services are held and what time you have them." I breathed deeply and tried, unsuccessfully I think, to tell him I was not afraid, although he could probably see my knees touching each other in regular motion. I told them the times of our services and they disappeared. Errol would become our youth leader and would see great growth in our youth group. Many of those young people are in ministry today.

Errol married a beautiful and godly girl Debbie. She was one of the lovely young people in our church. Her cousin Sharon, and her family were also in our church. Her Dad was one of our faithful church officers. He was one of the godliest men I have known. Sharon, would one day study with us at Africa School of Missions, meet her husband Clive, and today they serve God in a great church in Perth, Australia, which they had pioneered some years earlier. Errol and Debbie have planted a church in Jacksonville, Florida, and we have shared many wonderful and intimate moments with them in ministry. There are countless of these stories, too many to recount.

When we went to Fairview there was an old house attached to the church. It was in a state of bad repair and Paul started renovations on the house. Every Saturday, he went across to the church and worked on the building. There was always an early morning prayer meeting. After that he would stop at a little Portuguese bakery and buy a loaf of hot bread. He would come home with the steaming bread which we devoured before it had time to cool. After breakfast, he returned to the church to commence his work on the old house. We were doing other renovations on the church at that time and although there was money in the bank, one of the church officers refused to release the finance. Paul was in a pickle. He needed to pay one of the contractors who had been contracted for a special job on the building, and the officer said a simple: "No." All the renovations had been approved by the officers and Paul and some of the other men in the church had saved a lot of money by doing the work themselves. The church officer was rigid in his decision and said that the contractor was asking too much money and he would not release it.

All that we could do was pray. This was a Sunday evening and the contractor wanted his money on Monday morning. Paul has always had a strong conviction that our debts should consistently be paid on time. We were both feeling stressed. Those are the times when fear can settle on you like a cold ocean and you think you may drown beneath it. However, faith is greater than fear and we began to pray earnestly that God would answer our prayer. We were sitting at home with a friend who had preached in our church that evening. We were eating chocolate and drinking tea in the hope of consoling our hearts. Even the decadent sweetness of that Cadbury chocolate and the amber liquid running down our throats did not console us. Our friend said, "Goodnight," and went to bed. At midnight, the phone rang. When the phone rings at midnight fear takes on a whole new meaning. In that moment, fear crept up my legs into the pit of my stomach and rendered me motionless. I know Paul was also alarmed at a midnight call because when he answered the phone his voice had a tremble. I saw him moisten his lips as his salivary glands dried out and he answered hesitantly; "Hello, Paul speaking." I could see by his expression that the voice on the other side immediately put him at ease. The faintest smile began to play on his lips until it broadened into a generous smile. Suddenly the heavy and anxious feeling that filled the room lifted and I knew everything was okay.

Paul got off the phone and informed me that one of our faithful deacons had said; "I am going to leave a blank check under the pot plant on your porch. Whatever it is that is owing to the contractor, fill it out and pay for it." God never fails.

The church officers decided to build on to the parsonage as we were doing a lot of entertaining and we didn't have a guest room. They built a beautiful study for Paul and a lovely guest room with an en-suite bathroom. I was starting to wonder if building additions on to our home was a good idea. As the addition was nearing completion, life was about to take a twist and turn that neither of us had ever imagined.

It was a glorious Johannesburg morning, and as I stood washing dishes at my kitchen sink, I felt a deep contentment. My hands were all soapy, the children were playing outside and I was happy. Why wouldn't I be? Anna and Jay, were flourishing, the church was growing, the house had a brand-new extension, and we had managed to reserve a place for our children in two excellent schools. All our plans were neatly laid out for the next ten years. I was peering out my kitchen window, admiring the beautiful blue wisteria creeping up and relentlessly attaching itself to the side of my garage wall. It was in full bloom; the sun was shining and amber hues filtered through the tree tops leaving the earth bathed in a warm glow. I love nature, the sights, the sounds all fill me with joy. To complete the beauty of the moment, birds chirped happily as they nestled in the trees. The only word that I can think of that truly describes the day is that it was idyllic.

I was in my own happy world when Paul barged into the kitchen. He disturbed the beautiful moment in which I was soaking. He came up to me, grabbed my hand, took me down the passage, shoved me against the bedroom wall and said: "God spoke to me." I was startled for two reasons. Firstly, Paul never came home mid-morning. Secondly, this taking my hand, leading me down the passage, and putting my back against the wall was so unlike him. This was out of character for Paul. I knew whatever it was he had to tell me was urgent. Read on to find out about the next chapter of our lives.

Prayerful Pause:

In the greater scheme of things, our lives are fleeting and we have to pray that in the limited time of our mortality we will somehow produce meaningful fruit. I do not believe that anything we do is wasted; the meals we cook, the lyrics we wrote, the music composed, the poems we created, everything will count in the eternal realm. At times, we may feel insignificant but all Jesus asks is for is what we have in our hands, nothing more and no less. If we give Him what we have He can multiply it. Consider the story of Elisha with the twenty barley loaves. Elisha tells the man who brought the loaves to give it to the people to eat. The man knows the bread won't feed 100 men but he obeys and distributes the bread. Not only do they have enough to eat but there is bread left over. You can read the account in the second book of Kings. Ponder what happened to the disciples with a few small fish in their hands. God took what was in their hands and multiplied it, so that those few small fish and two loaves fed five thousand men. God is not looking for some amazing gift inside of you, He only wants what is in your hand. He requires obedience to His will. *Radical obedience,* is a call to one and all who claim to be disciples of Jesus.

Will you take time to pause now and pray? What can you offer the Lord? Have you a gift of hospitality? Honor God with that gift. Is your gift one of artistic talent? Allow God to use that talent for His glory. Whatever you have in your hand, allow God to take it and use it for the extension of His Kingdom. We have one life to live. It is only what we do for Christ that will last. Make a lasting impact with your life.

Chapter Thirteen

OBEDIENCE FOR GLOBAL IMPACT

· · · · · · · · · ·

Expect great things from God. Attempt great things for God

WILLIAM CAREY

PAUL

After just over two years serving as senior pastors of our home church, Fairview Assembly, a strange and inexplicable melancholy spirit settled on me. It was not evident to others. It was just a shadow on my soul. I knew it was not psychological and it certainly wasn't in any way some imbalanced chemistry in my brain. It was deeply spiritual, theologically confusing, and very unpleasant.

My preaching was as energetic as ever and I never doubted the content of my messages nor the absolute truth of the Bible. The church was growing, and we rejoiced in seeing ever increasing numbers of young people being discipled. But I would return home after a wonderful Sunday and feel a creeping despondency.

This internal conflict lasted for nearly six months. My office was on the upper level of an old house that stood behind the church. We had worked tirelessly to try to improve the place but it was still run down. I only had a part time administrative assistant and so there were some long and lonely hours spent keeping office hours and trying to prepare for the several services I preached at each week. It was during one of these long days that I breathed a desperate prayer. It was more of a groan than a prayer. I pleaded with God to let this shadow leave me.

To this day I am not sure of what happened was physical or spiritual or both. My only certain defense for the experience I had was that I know, because I know, because I know, that it was real. It felt like a bright light passed before my bookshelves. The room felt illuminated and I physically felt the presence of the Divine. I stood behind my desk with wide eyes hoping that the ecstatic moment would go on and on.

It soon passed but my heart was pounding and with an indescribable impulse and instinctively, I knew three things. Firstly, we would be leaving pastoral ministry. Secondly, we would impact nations, and thirdly, that we would trust God on behalf of others. None of these concepts had ever been rehearsed or previously considered. But I knew them to be the voice of God.

As quickly as this experience had occurred it was over but my heart was racing and I could not wait to tell Carol about it. I raced downstairs, drove home as fast as legally possible and ran excitedly into the house. Carol just stared at me as I grabbed her arm and pulled her down the passageway before literally pinning her up against the wall and declaring that I had no doubt that God was moving us into another dimension of ministry. Typically, she was immediately willing to be a part of whatever it was into which God was leading us. I also think she was simply very relieved that her husband had life and joy again.

By the following Friday I had a nervous feeling that the internal melancholy sensation that I had despised for the previous six months might be wanting to return. To ensure that it did not, I suggested that we take a day away to visit some dear friends who had recently moved to serve on the staff of a Christian guest farm. It was about a four-hour drive, but we piled into the car and left. They offered us kind hospitality but the deep question overshadowing the occasion, was what God was really trying to say.

Carol returned from the bathroom with a sense that God had spoken to her in the words of the book of Isaiah, that God's ways are higher than ours but there was little further clarity. We needed to leave the next day in order to be back for Sunday services in Johannesburg. Almost immediately the children fell asleep and all that we could hear was the quiet droning of the car. We rounded a sweeping bend in the road and for the second time in a week I was overwhelmed by the presence of God and sensed His voice.

I turned to Carol with wide open eyes and told her that God had told me what we were to do. It was that we would mobilize missionaries and send them around the world. In fact, we would start a school, and it would be called Africa School of Missions (ASM.) We arrived home and, as if by dictation, I wrote six pages of ideas. They were primitive and naïve, but I believed every bit of what I had written was possible.

We were so convinced by the experiences of the previous few weeks that we decided it was time for action. I had recently read a book by Lauren Cunningham, the founder of Youth With a Mission and he recorded several remarkable properties that had been given to the mission. We believed for the same. We returned to our friends on the Guest Farm and the following day walked confidently into a real estate agent's office. We informed him that we wanted to buy a farm. When asked what kind of farm, we said any would do; we would know if it was the right one. We even declared that cost was not an issue.

Our strategy was simple. As one of us kept the agent busy the other would walk away and passionately ask God for the property. When the next farm seemed to have better prospects, we prayed for that one as well! It was not long until we found what seemed to be the perfect farm. It had a very large house and we could imagine having eight to ten envisioned young people staying there and training to be missionaries. Just what they would learn we did not know.

We took the very audacious step to actually sign an offer to purchase. It was more naïve faith than *radical obedience* but we were too young to know the difference. Again, we made the four-hour journey home and arrived at our house to receive a phone call that the farmer had rejected our offer. We were incensed. This did not happen in the faith narratives that we had read so eagerly. As quickly as the vision burst to life it died. I remember handing it back to God in a rather defeatist way.

It was less than three weeks later that I received another phone call. There were no niceties or enquiries as to my health; it was a simple question wanting to know about my vision. It only took that little prompt and the vision was resurrected so, I shared it with enthusiasm. The gentleman on the other end of the call, went on to ask if he could come and see us.

Sensing something exciting, I invited him to dinner. Carol prepared a roast chicken and then we waited. An hour and a half after the agreed time he arrived with little by way of an apology. Carol was not happy at all. The dinner passed quickly, some cursory questions were asked, and he left. I did not have his contact number, knew very little about him and was left with a thought of just how strange this first encounter had been.

About ten days went by. Time was a little warped. Questions were swirling in my brain. Who was this man? Was God orchestrating something significant? I was put out of my uncertainty by a call in which our new friend asked if he could visit again and this time bring his wife. Carol quickly said that no dinner would be served but prepared instead a beautiful afternoon tea tray. Nevertheless, what started as a strange phone call and a subdued visit ended up by being a warm and fruitful friendship.

So, it was that our lives became deeply intertwined with Gerry and Mary Schoonbee. They are now both in heaven but you could not wish for better, nicer and more gracious people. Gerry was raised by a single Mom and went on to be a very successful engineer. He rose to the most senior role in Africa's largest road construction company. His background was Dutch Reformed. Mary was raised in Scotland in a devout Catholic family.

Some years before we knew them Gerry had been invited to a business leaders' breakfast. He was fifty-one years old and was deeply moved by the message and fully surrendered his life to Christ. He returned home a different man. The immediate problem he faced was that he could not tell Mary about his experience because they had made a strong commitment at the outset of their marriage that they would not discuss religion or politics.

The obvious change in his life made her insist that he share what had happened. As he did so her heart melted and she found what she had looked for throughout her life. She too became a fervent Christ follower. Very soon theirs was a journey of *radical obedience.*

They became extraordinarily generous with their resources. In our living room on the day that we got to meet Mary, they invited us to one of their properties. It turned out to be in exactly the same location as where we had been endeavoring to buy a farm.

It was October 1983, and we were once again on our way to White River, four hours east of Johannesburg. This time we drove through the gates of an elegant resort style hotel. As we entered the lobby our eyes gazed upwards to a soaring wooden ceiling that overlooked it, reaching an apex at least thirty feet above us. The views in every direction were spectacular and it was impossible not to be awed by the beautiful granite top of the Legegote mountain, that loomed above the property, in what is now Mpumalanga Province. We soon found out that the property had multiple reception rooms, a dining hall that could seat over one hundred people, a well-equipped kitchen, with walk in freezers, and fridges and laundry facilities. All of this, not to mention over thirty beautiful bedrooms, with attached bathrooms spread across fifty acres of land. There was a beautiful swimming pool and two brand new tennis courts. At the lower boundary of the property ran the Sand River, that fed a dam, making the view even more beautiful. Across the valley and only a few miles away was the famed Kruger National Park. It was idyllic and you couldn't ask for a better place for a training center.

The second day that we were there Gerry and Mary met with us in the lounge of the resort. Tea was served and a few final questions were asked of us. Then we heard what our ears could hardly believe. Gerry informed us that he and Mary had confidence in our vision. He went on to say that everything we could see, from the teaspoons in the kitchen to the tennis courts in the gardens were ours to do what God had called us to do.

By the time we made our way back to Johannesburg, it felt as though the car was floating. Our *radical obedience* had opened the way to establish a thriving and influential missionary training college. We worked hard during the following months. Soon we had resigned as pastors of Fairview Assembly and were trying to raise enough to live and raise our little family. We moved into two small rooms and had access to a borrowed car.

Using what few resources we had, we placed advertisements in Christian magazines. We recruited willing people to come and help us and in the final weeks cleaned every room, mowed most of the lawns and waited anxiously for the first students to arrive. Remarkably our first intake of students numbered thirty-six.

As most of this adventure was unraveling, my dear Dad passed away. I so wanted him to see the new campus but one of my last phone calls to him was from what would soon become my office on the campus. My two brothers, my younger sister, myself and our families said our final farewell to my Dad. We had lost my Mom only four years earlier. It was a surreal

Christmas that year. My sister was only fourteen when my Mom died and now we were all without our parents at a relatively young age. My Dad had been a certified accountant. Being born to stoic Scots parents and living through both the Great Depression and the Second World War, he had been financially conservative throughout his life. His affairs were left in meticulous order and we soon found out that each of us four children had a substantial inheritance coming our way.

It was not long before our sense of *radical obedience* was being challenged again. The question was: Did this vision for a missionary training center mean everything to us? If so, would we be prepared to give everything? With no hesitation, our answer was yes to both questions. So, it was that we took the entire inheritance left to us and invested it in the new establishment called Africa School of Missions. We have never regretted doing this. Some questioned us. One man even rebuked us, saying that the inheritance rightfully belonged to our children. But we did it anyway.

Several months later we pitched a very large tent on the campus and the evangelist Reinhard Bonnke addressed a crowd of nearly one thousand people there. The remarkable stories of God's provision over the following years are too numerous to record and only eternity will bare true witness to the faithfulness of God.

Allow me to share three significant highlights. Across the valley from our home was a growing number of unplanned villages that over time would burgeon into a sprawling settlement. Conditions were poor with no water or electricity. We had become involved in helping to develop water projects and so were familiar with our neighbors. We knew that *sangomas* or witchdoctors were active in these villages. They would pound on drums for hours at night.

One evening as we put little Anna in bed and began our evening prayer with her the drums seemed louder than before. They could be quite hypnotic in ways. Anna admitted to being afraid. We assured her that all would be fine and she laid down her head and slept. But I could tell that something was happening inside Carol's head. She eventually told me with deep and emotional conviction that she felt compelled to go the next day and find out where those drums were. I knew her well enough not to try to dissuade her.

The next day as I made my way across campus to my office Carol drove out, down the tar road and then turned onto the rough tracks that seemed to be the obvious area from where we were hearing those drums. She drove up and down those dusty tracks. She never did find a witchdoctor that day. What she did discover was dozens of very young children taking care of even younger children. She saw three-year-olds carrying their six-month-old siblings on their backs.

I returned home for lunch but Carol was not in the kitchen as was normal. I became anxious but then looked through the glass door of our living room to find her lying in the fetal position on the floor. I dropped down next to her with my first thought that she had been injured somehow. With tears pouring down her face, she told me of her experience that morning. Again, and again she repeated that we just had to do something.

Within days Carol had recruited a local lady to help. A very primitive village church was made available to her and she would load up our old Land Rover with water and whatever food she could find and make her way across the valley to care for the little ones. They would sing together. Often Carol and her helper would wash the matted hair of these precious small children. They had rest periods and soon the daily crowd of children grew to about two hundred.

The political climate was tense. Carol's work and even her life were threatened by activist thugs. The church was burned down and we discovered to our horror that the pastor had been poisoned. Over time others picked up the burden as HIV/AIDS began to ravage the area. Home-Based care projects were established, as well as an orphan care ministry and together these initiatives would go on to serve thousands of children. The work continues to this day.

Another story amongst the hundreds that could be told was catalytic in my life. I had no advanced degree at the time and so was desperately trying to teach eager students from the small repository of my limited knowledge. I was teaching a class on missions. About three weeks into the semester, I had completely run out of material. I decided that my students needed my honesty and so I admitted that there was very little else that I could teach them.

At the time, we had been hearing of growing numbers of refugees that had been making the hazardous journey from Mozambique to areas to our northeast. The missiological texts that we had been studying recorded that displaced people such as new urban dwellers, migrants and refugees were often very receptive to the Gospel.

I suggested that instead of us working through a text in the classroom we should put it to the test and actually make plans to try to find these refugee people. My students were understandably enthusiastic about this suggestion. Early the next morning we gathered in the car parking area, clambered into the old van that had been donated to the college and I drove eight happy students off to encounter hopefully some very receptive people.

We drove for several miles on the tarred road, turned off onto a dirt road and continued for some more miles. I'm not sure what we were hoping to find but there was nothing there. No tents, no United Nations feeding centers and worse still, no refugees.

I will never forget the moment I saw what appeared to be a small group of people out of the left side of the vehicle. Insensitively I turned hard off the little track and drove up to the group at far too high a speed. The vehicle and the little group were immediately covered by a dust of red African dust. As the dust settled, we alighted from the vehicle and made a most inappropriate approach to the group. There was a mother with three little children gathered around her. The only shelter they had was some sticks tied at the top and covered by a torn open plastic shopping bag.

I reached out my hand to greet her but soon realized that, despite the commotion we had caused, she was staring blankly ahead. It was a very awkward moment. Fortunately, a young man emerged from nearby bushes and was able to translate for us. Her story changed my life forever.

Tired of the rape and plunder to which she had been subjected in Mozambique and having lost her husband to the civil war, she determined to take her family to safety. She had been told of a potentially friendly place if she followed the setting sun. This apparently friendly place required her to walk for two days through the Kruger National Park, one of the largest wilderness areas in the world. Her story is too traumatic to be told here. She told us with no emotion whatsoever that on the second night as she gathered her little family under the spreading branches of an Africa acacia tree, she found herself surrounded by a yelping pack of hyenas. Again, with no emotion, she explained that in a desperate moment as she waved a branch as much as she could a large hyena lunged forward and grabbed the baby from her breast. She never saw her baby again and the next morning she took her three remaining children and walked the rest of the way. There was no refugee camp waiting for her, no welcome committee and we had found her in this state, resigned to almost certain starvation.

We were speechless. There was nothing that we could do. Fighting back waves of emotion we assured her that we would return the next day. We drove home through tears, with not a word being said. As we parted, after leaving the vehicle, we agreed to meet early the following day. I found an array of picks and shovels, some tarpaulins, and we loaded what we could into the vehicle soon after sunrise. We found the dear woman and her children exactly where we had left them.

They were grateful for the food we had brought and we soon dug a latrine for her and erected a tarpaulin surround. We called on others to help us and over several weeks this woman, along with many others, were being cared for by Christ-following people.

Soon I had recruited a doctor friend to devote his life to this cause; then we converted a vehicle into a mobile clinic and over all these years that work continues with literally thousands of lives saved and helped.

Allow me to tell one more story of our time at Africa School of Missions. We were growing rapidly and desperately needed more space. An administrative center, family apartments, and workshop space, were now all critically needed. I calculated how much money would be needed to accomplish these goals. There was no obvious donor and so I felt that in desperation we should borrow the money. I gathered my team in my office and told them of my plan and knew immediately that they were not prepared to trust me and get into debt.

I was discouraged and retreated to my office mumbling something about their faithlessness under my breath. As I was wallowing in self-pity the door burst open and Carol appeared with her blond hair waving behind her, she was going at such a pace. I was taken aback but she wanted to speak to me with real urgency. She told me how she had been in prayer at home and felt God had clearly spoken to her. She quoted a scripture from Isaiah chapter forty-five, regarding Cyrus the king. God's promise was that He would provide treasures stored in secret places and Carol was convinced that now this was a promise for us.

I was leaving to preach in the east of France the next day and so took courage that this meant that there would be souls saved. Carol was insistent that it was not souls but money. She was so persuasive that in a staff meeting at the end of the day, I wrote the Scripture on a white board and shared Carol's conviction. I know there was a skeptical group of people in that room.

I flew to Europe the following day arriving in Frankfort, Germany. Some friends were there to meet me. They immediately informed me that a friend had asked to have lunch. I explained that I had just walked off an international flight and was not looking very respectable. They insisted that I should keep the appointment and drove me across town.

The friend they were referring to was the well-known evangelist Reinhard Bonnke. He welcomed me and we sat down to an excellent lunch. I reported on all the good things happening at Africa School of Missions. Never once did I mention the events of the previous day nor of our urgent need to expand the facilities. As we concluded our meal, he wiped his mouth with a napkin and looked across the table with wide eyes. He said that God had just spoken to him. He went on to say that he felt he had to sow a seed into our ministry.

We returned to his office quickly and he made a call which I did not understand as it was in German. Soon his door opened and Reinhard was handed what looked like a check. He called his wife from the next-door office and presented the check to me. I discreetly placed it in a pocket. He was not pleased with this and insisted I should open the check and see how much it was for. I had never seen so many zeros in my life. It looked like a huge sum. Indeed, it was. By the time we had converted it into South African currency it was exactly the amount that I had asked our leaders to consider borrowing. There was much rejoicing and soon several new buildings were erected on our campus.

Ten years passed quickly. Hundreds of other remarkable events took place. Young graduates were serving in forty-two nations around the world. ASM became a catalyst for mission in post 1994 South Africa, when Nelson Mandela became President of a united nation. A faithful God had honored our *radical obedience* and the foundation for a life committed to ministry training was laid. We left a thriving college and made our way to Australia.

Prayerful pause:

Faith, God's will and timing can at times seem out of order. If they are not lining up at this point in your life, I hope our story encourages you to remain faithful and patient. I know God is working out something more than you can see or even believe for. Prayerfully let God know of your willing heart and quiet obedience and He will work your situation out for good.

God loves to surprise us because He is God. We have both learned that God is infinitely cleverer than we are and His ways always supersede our ideas. *Radical obedience* also demands trust in a God who will lead you every step of the way. The Psalmist reiterates that our steps are ordered by the Lord. The Psalmist also said that every one of our days is ordained by the Lord, and they are written in His book. That is an amazing thought my friend. Pause and ponder for a moment. God has your life in view. He is watching over your steps and for all those who love, trust, and live in obedience, He will direct each and every step taken. Stop now and thank Him for His hand on your life.

Chapter Fourteen

OBEDIENCE DOWN UNDER

· · · · · · · · · · ·

It is our part to seek, His to grant what we ask: ours to
make a beginning, His to bring it to completion; ours
to offer what we can, His to finish what we cannot

St Jerome

CAROL

Our years at Africa School of Missions (ASM) can only be described as exciting, challenging, and inspiring. To see young people leaving the shores of South Africa, and serving in nations around the world, has and always will be the greatest joy for Paul and me. Nothing lights the fire in our hearts more than seeing beautiful, energetic, godly, young men and women answer God's call.

One of the other joys for me, at ASM, apart from investing in our students, was to serve in Kangwane, (a neighboring village) and minister to the very needy children of that community. I always had to drive to Kangwane in an old Landrover that someone had donated to the College. Driving from our beautiful campus, on Peebles Road, where ASM was located, to Kangwane, was always a challenge. As I drove, I would revel in the vibrant colors of flora and the amazing atmosphere of hope and orderliness that surrounded our campus. It rapidly diminished to dust and a sense of hopelessness as I neared Kangwane. Roads were always littered with bottles, crumpled newspapers, and dog feces.

Armies of children filed the streets, some with no clothing to cover their extended malnourished bellies resulting in kwashiorkor. Only a small handful of them were fortunate enough to be shabbily clothed with mismatched shoes. I really loved those beautiful children and with the help of a lovely Zulu lady who worked with me, we were able to share the love of Jesus with them, on a daily basis, for many months. A kind farmer always provided us with bananas to feed the children and we would carry gallons of fresh water for them to drink. One memory stands out clearly in my mind. A precious little boy, with kwashiorkor, only wearing a pair of torn shorts, no shirt or shoes, will always trouble me and remind me that there are children, precious souls all around the world who face hunger on a daily basis. This particular child, with haunting big brown eyes, was so incredibly hungry that he would devour the over ripe bananas skin and all. I know my words can never adequately paint the picture of that boy, but years later tears well up in my eyes and my heart aches for vulnerable children living without food, hope or care.

The atmosphere in that community was hopeless, infected with disease and poverty and the only way I could respond was to try to impact those children with the hope of Jesus. We worked in Kangwane until danger hindered us from further entry to that community.

Never regard the poor or homeless as lazy or ignorant; because lingering beneath the external, one often finds brokenness and dysfunctional homes that led to this desperate place. As humans, we can be quick to judge others but if we have not walked in their shoes or lived their story our opinions can be seriously flawed. These are broken people, and truth be told, we are all broken and that is why we need Jesus to make us whole again, to put us back together, and make things right. Unless we are willing to walk alongside the poor, helpless, and homeless, our judgments are unwarranted.

In the midst of great blessing and growth at ASM we got a call to go to Australia to lead Glad Tidings Tabernacle, based in Fortitude Valley, Brisbane. The church has a rich history, and was founded by William

Booth Clibborn in 1931. It soon became the largest Assembly of God church in Australia, and planted other churches in Brisbane and around the world. The church had a huge impact and ministered to the needy in the city. Today the church is called *Hope Center* and continues to flourish under the leadership of the Superintendent of Australian Christian Churches, Wayne Alcorn.

We went to Glad Tidings in January 1994. Leaving ASM, and my family, was heart wrenching. We both still love the continent of our birth, and we are grateful for the generosity of our Board at Trinity, who allow us to serve students in Africa. My wonderful parents had been with us at ASM from the beginning. They can only be described as genuine servants. Dad saved the College thousands of rands every year. He befriended farmers and business men and they generously donated food and construction materials over the years. Dad was winsome, and his outgoing and friendly nature won many friends for the school. Mom cooked the food for the students and faculty and she served the College faithfully with a happy heart and a perpetual smile for all those years. I am blessed to have had parents with big hearts, generous spirits, and willing hands.

My brother Geoff had been the Dean of Students since the College began in 1985. He married one of our students Karen White. They stayed on at ASM and Geoff served the College as the President for the next eighteen years. Geoff and Karen would later go to India and serve as missionaries there for fifteen years.

On a scorching hot morning, our family arrived in Brisbane, Australia. A large group of people from the church came to the airport to welcome us to our new country and home. As we stepped off the plane, early morning, waves of heat hit us as the shone beat relentlessly down on us. Like South Africa, homes were never air conditioned back then and neither was the church building. We would soon become accustomed to the overwhelming humidity and heat and learned to love the beautiful city to which God had brought us.

The church bought us a beautiful home in Albany Creek and we lived happily there for three years. Anna and Jay were in school and although Anna loved school Jay was never very happy in the learning environment. Jay was diagnosed with ADHD (Attention deficit, hyperactivity disorder,) and he found learning a challenge. Years later Jay conquered his disability and went on to study and complete his BA degree in Cultural Anthropology. He made some good friends, and one particular friend was Mark Leung, with whom Jay traveled around Europe. They made some wonderful memories on that trip and have remained steadfast friends. Anna had a wonderful circle of friends. Kersten Walcott, was specifically close to Anna and they also traveled around Europe together and had many wonderful adventures. Kersten was a regular visitor to our home in the USA when we moved there.

One day, we were driving to the store and a few streets from our home, in the same neighborhood, we saw a "For sale" sign outside a large plot of land. We stopped and walked around the land and felt an inclination to pray about building a home on that piece of land. We had lived in the church house for three years and feeling that it was time to buy our own home in Australia. After much prayer and making sure our finances would work, we purchased the piece of land. We then found a Christian builder who helped design our home. At that point, my parents had left South Africa and were living in Australia with us. We were anxious to add on a separate apartment where they could live and give them their own privacy and independence.

We built a beautiful home. Paul and I had fun dreaming and designing it. At that time, we believed we would be living there for the next thirty years. We thought about everything including grandchildren running around the house. We had a large piece of land with a lovely stream at the end of our property. We had a big, beautiful deck that overlooked gum trees with all the beautiful Australian birds perching in their branches. There were pink cockatoos, galahs, parrots, and a plethora of laughing kookaburra.

There has to be something about us building extensions onto homes, and worse than that, building a home from scratch. No sooner had we moved into our home than God began to stir our hearts. Here is what happened.

Paul was leaving on a ministry trip to Europe and he would be away from home and church for two weeks. At that point neither of us had any inclination as to what God would do in our hearts. Remember we had just moved into our home and we were loving every minute of being there.

Our family were all feeling settled and Mom and Dad were loving their beautiful apartment.

I was sitting on our balcony early one morning, enjoying the beauty of the hour. Sunlight was filtering through the trees, spreading dappled shade across the grass. The birds were causing a commotion in the trees as kookaburra laughed, parrots whistled and squawked while the galahs, the noisiest of all the birds, chirped and screeched relentlessly. I loved the cacophony of bird sounds. The sounds captivated me as I tried to identify the different birds in the trees. I sat with Billy Graham's autobiography *Just As I Am* on my lap; I was distracted from the contents by the cacophony filling my ears. I distinctly remember thinking: "We are so blessed to be settled and have a beautiful home to live in for the next number of years." I was thinking of the children. Jay was on his European adventures and Anna had started studies at the University of Queensland. My parents were also loving their beautiful apartment, which was just perfect for the two of them.

In the midst of the noise I felt God speak to my heart. I distinctly heard; "Do you love me more than this." I brushed the thought away thinking that all the noise was messing with my head. Again, I heard with more clarity; "Do you love me more than this house." Was this the Lord speaking to me? Was I hallucinating from the cacophony of bird sounds? A third time I heard distinctly in my spirit; "Do you love me more than this home?" I answered the voice in my head; "Lord, I love you way more than this home." Then I heard that still, clear voice say: "I am calling you to leave this all behind and serve my purpose in the nations." I felt a wave of excitement fill my heart. I was ready for an adventure. Then I pondered about my parents and my heart nearly stopped beating. We simply could not leave my parents after building them this beautiful apartment. We had only lived in our home for six months. What I failed to realize was that if God called us, He would most certainly take care of all the finer details.

Many years ago, when ministry was quite new to us, I recall sitting down and having a meal with a number of Pastor's wives. Most of them were from our sister denomination, the Apostolic Faith Mission of South Africa. I recall feeling fairly intimidated by these beautifully dressed and dignified women. I honestly felt like a very ordinary girl in their midst.

They began speaking about their lovely homes and how much they loved them. I recall one of them said; "Well, my husband must never tell me we are moving because if he does, I will tell him to go on his own." The other women nodded in agreement and they all seemed to feel quite strongly that the place they were was the place they would stay. I know it might seem like a trivial conversation and it probably was but it troubled me deeply. The words kept going around in my mind. I recall that I felt so distressed by their attachment to material things that I prayed a very earnest prayer. I said: "Lord, help me to hold loosely to the things of this world so that if you ever call us somewhere else, I will be willing to let go and obey you." It was one of those profoundly meaningful prayers and a decision I made that would help me with my choices in the years that followed.

I had no idea of the import of that prayer. I did not know where God would lead us and take us. I can say that in every home into which I have moved, I have echoed that prayer again. "God help me to hold things loosely." Has that prayer been challenged? Yes, when we moved to the States some years later our container was broken into and we had twenty-seven thousand dollars' worth of goods stolen as well as damages. Paul, looked at me and waited for the tears to come. No tears, I had prayed a prayer as a very young wife and I determined that it was not worth shedding tears over things.

Paul got home from his trip and as usual we made a pot of tea and went out onto our beautiful deck to sip our tea and talk about his trip. I could tell Paul was a bit anxious and knew there was something he wanted to tell me. I said to him; "Can I tell you what I feel God has been saying to me?" He quickly encouraged me to go ahead as I think it was a relief to him and gave him a bit of time to gather his own thoughts. I told him the story of my moments on the deck and how God had spoken to my heart about us serving His purposes in the nations. He looked at me, smiled, and said: "Well, that made my conversation a whole lot easier." While Paul was ministering away elsewhere, God had told him clearly, that he had finished his work in Australia and was now calling him to a life of faith and obedience. We would be serving the nations, living without a salary again and walking in *radical obedience.*

The next morning Paul went to the church offices and found a thick envelope that had been pushed underneath the door. The envelope was marked for Paul and Carol Alexander. He opened the envelope to discover a sum of six and a half thousand dollars. That was the first time we had ever received a personal gift in Australia and it was as if God used this to affirm that He would be our source and provider in this new walk of faith. As if that wasn't enough, a few weeks later we received another envelope containing three thousand dollars. No one knew we were leaving; but God did and He was showing us, in no uncertain terms, that He would provide for us and look after us.

Telling my parents was probably the most difficult part of the whole process. I was shaking when Paul went upstairs to their apartment to talk to them. Mom and Dad listened intently and told Paul that they would never interfere with what God was doing in our lives and that they would happily release us to His call. My parents were the most phenomenal, generous and giving people. They would move in with my older sister Gaille and her husband Vaughn and live in a little apartment built on the side of their house.

Our years at Glad Tidings were happy ones but we always knew in our hearts that we were only there to turn the church around and then move on to what was deeply embedded in our hearts: training men and women to touch the world with God's love. We had so many wonderful people and friends who made our time there joyous. Tim and Wendy Bean lived up the road from us and their home was a haven to our family on many occasions. We had a wonderful friendship which continues to this day. There were many amazing people who made life happy and we always reflect on our time in Brisbane with joy. We ate meals in each other's homes and people like Kevin and Yvonne James, Paul and Marie Giffin, Barry and Del Corless, Tom and Thelma Wright, and a host of other people, bring back memories filled with joy of their kindness and support through our years at the church. We left with heavy hearts as a group bid us farewell when we left some seven years later.

We left Australia in August 2000, and moved to the city of Chicago, where we served as missionaries in residence in Steve and Vickie Warner's church in Oakbrook. They were kind and hospitable and we loved our time in the little mission house on the side of the church. During that time, we launched a ministry called *Prepare International,* with the primary goal of helping to train Eastern European pastors to understand the biblical mandate of the Great Commission. We were living entirely by faith and of course there were never any offerings in Eastern Europe. However, God was so good to us and He used many people to bless us in our journey of faith.

One day a couple invited us out for a meal. They told us they had a burden for France and Europe and we thought we were going to this meal to encourage them to be missionaries. We had a wonderful time inspiring them about missions and at the end of the meal they handed Paul an envelope. He was quite surprised as we were simply going to inspire their hearts with regard to missions. There was four thousand dollars in that envelope; it was totally unexpected and very much needed. That couple supported us so generously over the next number of years and without their generous giving our ministry could never have thrived as it did. Hudson Taylor's words echo in my head, "God's work done in God's way will never lack God's supply." We have always found this to be true.

We eventually moved from Chicago to the lovely town of Concord, in North Carolina. God provided miraculously for us to buy a home and we had some very happy years living in Concord. We served with Sam and Vickie Farina for a number of months while still traveling and ministering in Europe. We were still working with *Prepare International* and it was going well until Paul went on a preaching trip to South Africa and once again everything turned upside down and inside out.

Paul was teaching at our College in South Africa, when he got a call from a church leader who served as a Governor (trustee) of the British Assembly of God Bible College. Of course, this college was our Alma Mater and Paul was surprised when he was approached about the possibility of being the new President. When Paul came home and told me about the invitation to take on the College, my immediate response was incredibly negative. As young people, we had endured such abuse from the senior pastor we had worked with that I could not even begin to entertain the idea of going there. Paul has always been patient with me and he suggested that we spend some time fasting and praying about the situation. I thought it was a waste of time and energy because I had not the slightest inclination of going to work back in the UK. However, the entire process went on hold because our son Jay was involved in one of the most horrific car accidents. Our lives would be forever changed.

Prayerful Pause:

It is my belief, that God calls every one of us as Christ followers to impact the world with His love. Christian character is so important in our walk. God wants to shape us and form us to become the people He wants us to be. The truth is, when we come to Jesus and our hearts are transformed, we become more like Him and in so doing we become who He truly created us to be. In a world full of folly, we need wisdom so that we can navigate these uncertain times with a certainty that comes from the knowledge that God is in absolute control. What the world needs is hope and the Christian message is exactly that. The greatest reason for our hope is the resurrection of Jesus from the dead. No other religion can ever make such a claim.

We all have a vital role to play in the world. God needs each and every one to play their part in seeing His kingdom come on earth. In other words, we are all called to fulfill His mission on earth. If you feel insignificant or that your life is meaningless, let me assure you that your heavenly Father does not view you in that light. You are His creation, made in His image, and He has a plan and a unique purpose for your life. Pause now and ask Him to reveal His plan for your life. Hold loosely to the things of the world because sometimes material things can be a distraction from serving the cause of Christ in our world.

If you have felt discouraged in your Christian walk, may I encourage you to keep going. As Hebrews 12 exhorts us, keep your eye on the goal. Take time to bow your head in submission and ask the God of all grace to strengthen you and uphold you. He will not fail.

Chapter Fifteen

OBEDIENCE THROUGH
TRAUMA

· · · · · · · · · ·

What grace is meant to do is to help good people, not to
escape their sufferings, but to bear them with a stout
heart, with a fortitude that finds its strength in faith

AUGUSTINE OF HIPPO

PAUL

The first day of July 2002 will live forever in our memory. At about lunch time there was a knock at our front door. We were living in Concord, North Carolina at the time. Carol was alone at home and the news she received was what no parent ever wants to hear. Our 22-year-old son Jason had been involved in a horrific car accident.

With a trembling voice that I hardly recognized, Carol called to let me know. We rushed to the Carolinas Medical Center. It took nearly two hours of agonizing waiting before we were told that he was still alive but was in emergency surgery. Sometime later some ashen faced doctors called us into a little room and delivered the worst news. We were told that people with Jason's injuries do not survive and we should prepare for the worst.

Jason's car had been smashed by a fully laden garbage truck traveling at about sixty miles per hour. The impact was so great that it pushed the car about one hundred and twenty yards, mounted the sidewalk, destroyed two trees and then rolled over on top of it.

The details are far too numerous to list, and Carol has told the full story in her book *Wild Hope: A Memoir*. What we found out was that Jason had been airlifted to hospital with virtually every rib smashed into small pieces and massive internal injuries. Most internal abdominal organs had been crushed. Just one of his injuries was a ruptured aorta; an injury that results in death in over 90% of cases.

By late that same night, we were ushered into the trauma intensive care unit ostensibly to say our final farewell. We could hardly recognize our boy. Large quantities of fluid had been pumped into his body to help compensate for the massive bleeding. He had received so much blood, platelets, and frozen plasma that it equated to over six full blood transfusions. Just the amount of foreign material in his body should have killed him. We could not see the huge wounds where his back had been opened in order to perform the life-saving surgery. By the time we saw him after his surgery he had gained nearly eighty pounds from all the fluids that had been pumped into him.

Our long, dark, and agonizing journey continued day after day. I would rise by 5.00 am and nervously call the trauma ward to hear any update. Not a day went by without us being told it was likely Jay's last. After I had made a cup of tea I would climb the stairs and tell Carol he was still alive and we could keep believing despite the dismal reports we were receiving from the team of doctors caring for Jay. Day after agonizing day, we were told that Jay was on the verge of death. I am telling the story briefly but it is a miraculous story. Jay was a G3 at the accident scene, which meant there was no breathing, no pulse, and no visible sign of life. The doctors prepared us for the worst.

On the twenty first day, he opened his eyes. Because there was no blood to feed his spinal column during surgery the doctors were convinced that he would never walk again. To everyone's delight he could wiggle his toes and was cognitive enough to pull out his tongue when asked. Despite contracting deadly hospital viruses, continuing to suffer from a hole in his heart where a rib had penetrated it, and having most of his muscle mass gone, Jay was finally transferred to a rehabilitation hospital. We were told to expect months of rehabilitation. In fact, it turned into only about ten days and the doctors informed us that he would most likely regain strength better at home

We drove home that day and it felt as though we were bringing a newborn into the house. I wanted the whole neighborhood to see us coming home and I am sure I beamed from ear to ear. But it was not easy. He could hardly put one foot ahead of the other. Each day was a small victory and Carol and Anna provided incredible love and care. I would support him as he walked across a room. Eventually we got down the path to the mailbox. By October he recovered enough to return to hospital to have the hole in his heart repaired. After that he regained strength rapidly.

By the end of that year, we felt confident enough to reopen conversations regarding us serving the Bible College and Graduate School in the UK. Leaving Anna and Jay in the US was hard but we had another problem. Despite having a good health insurance plan (Jason's hospital bill came to well over $800,000.00), we were receiving a bill for $36,000.00. I kept asking for details but none were forthcoming and so we withheld payment. In reality, we could not have seen anyway to pay this huge sum anyway. Eventually our health insurers set up a three-way call with the hospital and to our shock and dismay we found that this huge amount was for blood and blood products, none of which were covered by insurance. We were liable for full payment.

We committed the matter to prayer. In fact, we would receive rather nasty calls from debt collectors at all hours of day and night. On one such call the caller offered to settle for $20,000.00 if I made a commitment immediately. I was so taken aback and before I knew what I had said I asked if he would allow me to pray about it. He was so shocked he said sure and hung up.

Nevertheless, we felt the weight of this debt especially in the light of our move to England. We shared our problem with one of our dearest friends, Becky Hammett. She was a senior administrator in a medical practice, and we knew should would have some insight to our problem. She called the hospital. The person who checked Jay's record came back and expressed her sympathy thinking that Jason must have died. After careful negotiating and several calls Becky, was thrilled to inform us that the hospital would settle for just $5,000.00. We were relieved beyond words.

A week later, we made a preliminary trip to England, preparing for our move sometime later. A dear friend who pastored a church in Leicester had invited us to preach on the Sunday we were there. I like to be on time, and it was frustrating that we were held up in traffic and arrived as the worship had already begun. Our friend met us in the foyer and asked that instead of preaching could we please tell Jason's story. Their church had prayed earnestly during our painful ordeal. We were glad to do so, and the church responded with great joy as we shared of our son's recovery. As I was about to take my seat Carol caught my attention and said that I should tell the last part of the miracle, that of the bill being cut so dramatically. I did so and felt gratitude fill my heart again as I shared.

After the service, a young couple moved quickly in Carol's direction. I could see them sharing something in a very animated way. Soon Carol called me over and asked them to tell me their story. It transpired that the young lady had lost her grandmother some weeks before. They learnt that they were to receive an inheritance and had determined to give a tithe of the total away. They had prayed about who or where to give it to. On their way to church they had felt that God was telling them that He would show them what to do. After hearing me tell our story they felt compelled to let us know that they wanted to give this money to us. We had no idea how much it was, but we quickly involved their pastor and told them to get his blessing. The pastor was delighted and when the final amount came through it was exactly what we needed to clear our debt. The long, painful and yet miraculous journey was over.

A few months before leaving for England I received a note from our health insurer. It informed me that I was due for a "well man's checkup." I thought this was very strange. Sick men do not want to go to the doctor so would a healthy man want to? I ignored the note until Carol found it a few days later. She went on to say that if I loved her and the children I would go for the check. I did so but with a very bad attitude.

I was not impressed by the doctor and impolitely informed him that he did not need to check my pulse because I would not be in his office if I did not have one. We went through the normal routine of a checkup and then he recommended that I go to the hospital for a stress test. Again, I was not impressed but knew it was what Carol would want and so made my way to the hospital.

All went well until they ramped up the treadmill, got my heart racing and then quickly lay me down to conduct a scan. That was when the cardiologist thought he had identified a bicuspid aortic valve. He said he could not be sure but I should keep my eye on it.

Soon after arriving in England, I registered with a doctor's office and told the general practitioner of my experience during the stress test. He assured me that people die *with* a bicuspid aortic valve not *from* one. However, he suggested that I should get to see a heart specialist. This began about a year's worth of doctors' visits and one scan after another.

Eventually a letter arrived informing me that there was an abnormality with my aorta and I should report to the Sheffield General Hospital for a trans-esophageal scan. Without any anesthetic, a camera was rammed down my throat and manipulated for about twenty minutes.

The gag reflex kicked in and I struggled to handle the sensation. All the time a rather unattractive nurse was shouting at me every time my hands ventured near the cable connected to the camera. It felt like an eternity but eventually the camera was extracted, and I lay trying to recover. The doctor who had performed the procedure asked if I had any pain. I assured him that I did not, and he went on to tell me that my aorta—the main artery exiting my heart, was seriously at-risk due to a very large aneurism. Basically, I had a bubble the size of an orange, extending the artery. The danger was that it could burst at any moment. This would result in almost instant death.

Further tests revealed that this bubble had extended past the junction to the carotid artery making potential surgery extremely difficult and dangerous. Due to the pressure on the hospital system in England it took ten long months from diagnosis until surgery.

I reported to the hospital. It was an old Victorian building with large, mixed wards. In the bay where I was placed were six men all much older than me. When I asked them what they were in for I was told that most were having bypass surgery and that the procedures would last about three hours. Even at this late-stage I thought mine would be a relatively simple procedure.

Later that evening the anesthetist came by to see me. Carol was sitting on the side of the bed when he began to describe the severity of the operation. He explained that it could take fifteen hours. When I asked why, his answer was most distressing. He said that they would take some time to open me up. The they would "put my blood in a bucket and close me down." This sounded very primitive, and I asked for further explanation. He explained that they could not perform the procedure on a beating heart and the size and location of the aneurism meant that I could not be placed on a bypass machine. So, they would stop my heart and have at the most twelve minutes to remove the aortic aneurism, replace it with a prosthetic one, replace the aortic valve, and then suture up all the arteries that serve the heart muscle itself. Then they would restart my heart and slowly warm me up to prevent shock.

I could see Carol's eyes wide open in horror. I was spared any further distress by having three sleeping pills given to me and, apart from a very groggy hug and kiss with Carol the next morning the next I knew I was waking up in intensive care many hours later. Carol's first visit was very traumatic as it brought back so many memories of us seeing Jason through his post-accident recovery. Four days later I was wheeled back into the large ward. It was not a pleasant experience in any way.

After eight days, I was allowed to go home. They packed up medications and gave me a little pillow to hug to my chest that had a line of stitches running down its entire length. In front of my right shoulder was a long line of stainless-steel staples that were closing the wound where the surgeons had set up an alternative blood supply to my brain while performing the surgery. Weakness prevailed but I managed to gingerly walk out of the hospital and sat in the back seat of our car while Carol drove very carefully and slowly out of Sheffield.

Sheffield is a large industrial town famous for steel and even more so for high quality cutlery. Although the products made there are beautiful the skyline of the city is certainly not. Soon we were leaving the industrial landscape behind and driving into the lush green fields of South Yorkshire.

The fields were lined with beautiful and well-trimmed hedgerows. In many of the fields there were ancient oak trees, verdant meadows and beautiful sights. I found myself being overwhelmed with emotion. My eyes were hungry, and I looked intently at sights I had probably seen a thousand times without ever really noticing them. Then I glanced forward and saw the most beautiful sight of all. Concentrating on making the ride as smooth as possible I saw the glowing and beautiful blond hair of the bride of my youth. I was going home. My mind raced. I would see my children (who had come to England to support us during this time.) I believed I would see my children's children. The call of God would remain upon my life. I was completely overwhelmed and wept silently as we made our way home.

It took three long months to recover but eventually strength returned. Soon I was back in the classroom and leading the College. Life would never be the same again and I was changed for the better. I valued things that were unimportant before. My precious wife and family were everything to me. The privilege of preaching has never left me since that time. God had been faithful and what almost certainly would have shortened my life, perhaps catastrophically, was now behind us.

Jason's accident and my surgery were things that always seemed to happen to other people. Our family had been spared trauma until these two events occurred. We learnt the importance of having a comprehensive theology. God is not only the Lord of the good times but He is comforter in the bad times. We live this side of heaven and bad things do happen to good people. We became more tolerant, hopefully kinder, and gentler, and certainly grateful for every day. Every morning, when Carol and I wake up, we hold hands and express our gratitude to God for His goodness before anything else.

Prayerful Pause:

We have shared our story of trauma many times. Sometimes it is so difficult as we know we are speaking to people who have had at least an equivalent level of trauma and, in many cases, outcomes were far worse. Petty answers and superficial sympathy are so empty. The only reasonable response to trauma of any kind is to decide our response. It requires faith because bitterness and anger will only add to the pain. Deep surrender to the love of an eternal God, who knows the end from the beginning, is the only sure way to find peace and comfort amid trauma. I urge you to pray. Pray with quiet surrender, pray with deep conviction, and pray for grace to see God work things together for your good. I do not consider it even the slightest level of defeat to acknowledge that some things are only fully resolved at the resurrection when Jesus will reveal everything. It is then that we cease seeing through a dark glass and will worship with full hearts, the God who was, and who is, and who is to come. My prayer, as I write this, and you read it, is that the God of all comfort will comfort and keep you.

Chapter Sixteen

OBEDIENCE YIELDS GOOD FRUIT

· · · · · · · · · ·

*Resolution One: I will live for God. Resolution
Two: If no one else does I still will*

Jonathan Edwards

PAUL

Our move to England was challenging in many ways. Jason's accident had
put everything in our lives on hold. Anna was at university and opened
her heart one evening as to her apprehension about us living abroad while
she remained in the US with no close relatives at all.

As we faced our challenges on the home front, we were deeply
committed in two other areas. The first was a missional commitment to
Europe. For years I had served with my dear friend Ian Green (we were
roommates in college), who had pioneered many leadership development
initiatives to the former Eastern bloc. The needs in these Eastern European
counties seemed overwhelming as they emerged from decades of Soviet
control. We felt a theological and spiritual ache in our hearts and wanted
to do something about it. We formed a small mission called "Prepare
International" and began offering a very basic training to these Eastern
European leaders reinforcing the biblical mandate for mission.

The second area of commitment was to our alma mater to which we were now being invited to serve. The British Assemblies of God had a long history of Bible College training. Starting in Hampstead in London in 1919, the first Bible College was formed. It later moved to the leafy suburbs in a place called Kenley in Surrey. Entire generations of Assembly of God pastors were trained there.

In the late 1960's London property prices were booming. Several Christian ministries were deciding to sell their properties in the greater London area and move to the industrial north where property was much more affordable. The Governors of Kenley Bible College decided to do the same. Another potential campus had been identified in North Nottinghamshire, about one hundred and fifty miles to the north. A combination of suddenly plummeting prices in a global property collapse and poor negotiations resulted in the northern property being bought and the sale on Kenley falling through.

By the time we went to college in the north, in a small village called Mattersey, the financial future of the college was tenuous. Students were restricted to one shower a week and possibly two hours of heating in the dormitories per day. Food was poor and I got very sick with the doctor telling me it was the result of malnutrition. Nevertheless, we loved our college years and the invitation to return as President was a high honor.

The college had enjoyed twenty-seven stable years under the steady leadership of Dr David Petts. New accommodation had been built and a state-of-the-art education building which incorporated a beautiful chapel had also been added. Mattersey Hall was by now considered one of the premier Pentecostal institutions in Europe.

We were soon expanding graduate programs, offering European leaders opportunities to gain a great education, and serving in places as far afield as Malaysia and South Africa. Over a few years we were able to gather an extremely gifted and talented faculty. Biblical languages, missiology and systematic theology were strengths in our curriculum. We pioneered a very successful Master of Arts program. We called it the MA in Missional Leadership. We were the first in the world to use this nomenclature, but it was soon adopted elsewhere.

We would offer intensives over weekends at the Hilton Hotel in Sheffield. Among the extraordinary joys was having the entire executive leadership of the Irish Christian Churches complete the degree with us.

Doors opened around the country and Carol and I were seldom home over weekends as we served churches from north to south. I was privileged to serve on the National Leadership Team. Those were rich and very happy years.

After nearly seven years, our fellowship had a change in its national leader previously known as the superintendent. I had helped facilitate this change but soon began to sense that all was not well. Snide remarks by the national leader at a graduation ceremony and other signals made me feel most uncertain.

Most of my fears were soon realized and we knew that our time in the United Kingdom was coming to an end. Soon we were left with no choice, and our happy and fruitful time came to a rapid termination. It was devastating but some of our most faithful friends stood by us in remarkable ways. Ken and Christine Williamson from Dagenham in London were simply amazing in their kindness and support. Iain and Elizabeth Duthie from Aberdeen in Scotland met us in Edinburgh and showed us overwhelming generosity. We can never forget these gracious, kind and generous friends. There were many others as well.

It became clear to us that we should return to America. We arrived back in the US with no idea at all of what the future held. This was not so much *radical obedience* as it was *raw obedience*. Not many weeks after arriving back we received a call inviting us to a small and obscure Bible College called Trinity situated in the insignificant town of Ellendale in North Dakota. Carol was very skeptical but I was happy to be active in ministry and so we planned an extension to a ministry trip that had taken us to Chicago. I completely miscalculated the vastness of the American prairies. It was mid-January and very cold. Everything looked bleak and lifeless, and we drove on and on.

Eventually we crossed the state line into North Dakota, drove another five miles north and turned right onto Main Street, Ellendale. As the pillars of Davidson Hall came into view, I felt my heart race, but my brain was determined to ignore the impulse.

What happened over the following two days is recorded in detail in Carol's memoir, but it is enough to say that we left that cold and lonely little town with a deep conviction that this was where God wanted us to serve. I consoled myself with thoughts of this just being a foothold before better and more prominent positions opened. It was minus nineteen degrees Fahrenheit as we drove away with a warm invitation to assume the presidency of Trinity Bible College.

In retrospect, the driving force in us accepting the role was nothing short of *radical obedience*. We had no employment contract, no actual offer of a salary and knew instinctively that the college was in bad shape. There was only one administrative leader left, the Dean of Students. I persuaded him to stay but three weeks later he resigned.

I reached out to a former graduate student of mine, Ian O'Brien. He and his family had emigrated to the US, and I invited him to serve as Dean of Students. In an act of obedience, he and his family moved to Ellendale. I will forever be grateful to Ian for those early years and his amazing support. Then there was Winston and Candyce Titus. They agreed to serve with us and were soon running the business office. Almost every day they uncovered unpaid bills and unrecorded debts. Yet their faith never wavered, and they faithfully worked with debtors to buy extra time.

Financial worries were not the only concern. Our accreditors had served us with a "show cause" notice. This is the worst of the various censures that accreditors can impose. Few colleges ever recover from this action. I was required to "make an appearance" before the Commission on Accreditation annually. I have often referred to this as the walk of shame. It was intense and difficult. Our faculty were rightly disgruntled and were somewhat skeptical of my leadership. A very long three years later I made that lonely walk one more time but, on this occasion, it was to the joyous news that our accreditation had been fully restored.

Then we added graduate programs, eventually leading to a substantial offering including multiple master's degrees, a Doctor of Contextual Leadership and a cutting edge, research-based Doctor of Philosophy (PhD). Generous donors became more deeply invested and on a single occasion pledged over three million dollars to our work.

A new prayer center was built because of one incredibly generous couple believing in our vision. The iconic Davidson Hall was entirely restored, to become a world class central administrative building. The women's dormitory was refurbished to a high standard and a complex of apartments bought. The President's house was returned to its 1905 glory, and we feel privileged to be its occupants.

Towards the end of our eighth year, we began to aggressively pay down debt because of one generous couple's kindness. The day we shredded the mortgage and were able to declare that we were completely debt free, was a joy, almost beyond description.

As outstanding as these and many other accomplishments are, they pale in comparison to the friends who have come alongside. Kind and loving people have been a thousand-fold reward, for any early struggles at Trinity or lingering disappointment from our time in England. Churches have flung open their doors, entire Districts have had us speak to their pastors again and again. The reward for *radical obedience* is beyond description and, given the opportunity, we would do it over again and again.

CAROL

Our time at Mattersey was drawing to a rather abrupt end. We had seven good years serving in the College and saw much fruit for our labor. There were some denominational challenges but they are not worth elaborating upon. What is worth mentioning, is that on the 31st of October 2011, I had a powerful dream. It was undoubtedly a prophetic dream and I knew instantly that it was from God. Paul shares that story in his book *Faithful: Stories of Trust, Courage, and Resilience;* however, it does bare some repetition for context.

There were two parts to my dream. The first portion of the dream described what we were leaving. The dream also gave me insight to why we were leaving. This portion of my dream came to pass over the following five years. It was undoubtedly a prophetic dream. In the second part of my dream, Paul and I were sitting in a car. Paul's hands were on the steering wheel but he wasn't driving. I suddenly became aware of something on the back seat. I turned around and saw what I perceived was a dead baby. I said to Paul: "The baby is dead." We both began to weep. I suddenly felt I needed to turn around and touch the baby, and as I did, the baby stirred and came to life. I picked up the baby to nurture it and said ecstatically: "The baby is alive, its alive." I then woke up from my dream.

It was 5.00am in the morning. I nudged Paul and said: "Love, I had a dream, I need to tell you about it." He replied sleepily: "Go back to sleep

131

darling." How on earth is a woman meant to get back to sleep after a dream like that? I tried to bring the dream up at breakfast but Paul didn't want to hear about my dream.

One of our daily rhythms of life is to have a cup of tea after lunch. We always ate in the College cafeteria, and then we would go back to our home, which was on the campus and make a cup of tea. I was sipping my tea still pondering this dream. I knew it was prophetic and had something to do with our future. I put my head back on the couch and said: "Lord, please tell me the meaning of my dream." I heard that soft, still voice answer me back: "It is your future ministry."

Now, you need to understand that I am an African girl, born and raised. In my view, a dream like that must mean we were going back to Africa to look after orphan children. People got wind of the fact that we were leaving Mattersey, and as the news disseminated, we received a flurry of invitations. One of those invitations was to help in a very significant ministry in Africa. There were also other appealing and lucrative invitations. None of them sat comfortably with us.

In early December, we returned to our home base in the United States. I was so happy to be home with our children and our church in Concord. Paul was feeling apprehensive about our future but I felt absolute peace that God had our future in His grasp and firm command; everything was going to be fine. That is when the phone rang. I call events like this, Divine interruptions. Paul answered the phone; there was a long pause, I heard some muffled words and then he came through to the kitchen where I was busy preparing our evening meal.

He looked at me somewhat skeptically and relayed the message: "There is a Bible College in a town called Ellendale, in North Dakota. It seems as if they are looking for new leadership; anyway, they have asked if we would go there and do a Spiritual Emphasis Week with their students." I looked at Paul quizzically and replied: "Where on earth is that?" He wasn't sure so he went to get the map book. For those young people reading this book, a map book is what the older generation used to find their way around the country. We didn't have Google maps and Navigation systems to find our way around. The map revealed a small town on the south-east corner of North Dakota. I immediately challenged the idea of going. Paul then suggested that we pray about the invitation. I didn't want to pray about this invitation because I knew I didn't want to go and I really didn't want to waste our time. There was no way that God would ever include us in His plan in this little town in a seemingly insignificant state. After all, I had prayed that our next position of ministry would be somewhere with palm trees, blue skies and white beaches. I knew that was Hawaii. However, I felt I should give the Lord a few options, so I said: "Okay, Lord if it is not Hawaii, then California or Florida will do just fine."

After much prayer, and some persuasion from Paul, I agreed to go and share the week of ministry. We were preaching in Chicago and so it seemed feasible to go further north to this town Ellendale. I did not realize how much further north we had to go. On the 19th January 2012, Paul and I were making the long trek to Trinity. I remember the weather was a freezing 19 degrees below zero. There was no snow on the ground so everything looked bleak and dismal. We finally arrived on the campus. The air was so cold but suddenly I felt a warm glow on the inside that I did not understand.

We were welcomed on to the campus by the Administration and we had a couple of interesting days. I remember the first chapel service at which we were speaking. After the vibrant worship at Mattersey, I found the worship at Trinity rather dry. However, when Paul got up to preach, the students were like sponges soaking in every word. It was amazing to see nearly the entire student body flock to the front in devotion to the call of God. They were beautiful young people. The following day I preached and the response was similar. These young people had a somewhat conservative exterior but they loved Jesus passionately.

After the second day, we were invited into a small conference room to meet with some of the Board. We had not realized that some of the Trinity Board members had come to assess us. We sat in uncomfortable silence for a few minutes and then conversation began to flow. At one stage, the Chairman of our Board said that we needed to understand that the Board had seriously considered closing Trinity. He then surprised us by saying: "We thought the baby had died, but we felt that if someone would pick it up and nurture it, there was still life in it." Those words were the exact words I had used to explain my dream to Paul and to three other trusted friends and colleagues in the UK. My dream was so powerful and so obviously from God, that I had shared it with our best friends Ken and

Christine Williamson, as well as David Shearman and Phil Jones. I knew the Chairman had never spoken to any of these people and so even if he didn't realize then, he was prophesying and foretelling our future. I knew without a shadow of a doubt that this was where God wanted us. I had prayed for palm trees and blue seas but God knew what my heart really wanted.

What can I say about the last thirteen years? They have been the most wonderful and fulfilling years of our lives. In our early days, there were many financial challenges, faculty and staff challenges, and buildings were in an advanced state of deferred maintenance. But we loved where God had called us. The Lord was gracious in sending Winston and Candyce Titus to serve alongside us and in the three years they were here, they brought financial stability and supported us in unimaginable ways. They are the dearest of friends and we will always be grateful for the significant part they played in our early years.

In 2014, we started our first Graduate program at Trinity, and Paul asked me to lead the charge. Scott Townsend joined me in those early days and he still serves with me today. He has had health challenges along the way but is a servant in every sense of the word and the Graduate School would not be where it is without him. I have been supported by the most wonderful team of people. We serve joyfully together and enjoy so much fun at the same time. Everyone in our building knows that we are the rowdiest bunch because there is always raucous laughter emanating from my office. Without ChristyAnn Medley, and her joyful spirit, the Graduate School would not function. God also blessed me by bringing fellow South African, Noel Sanderson to work alongside me. The list goes on with David Bennett joining the team in the last couple of years and bringing with him a quiet dignity that has done nothing to stifle the other noisy members of the team. Others have come in the last couple of years and joined ChristyAnn in the administration of the programs. This team is God's team and I have been blessed to serve with them all.

The Graduate School continues to grow with students from over 30 countries around the world. God has been good, faithful, and so kind. The journey to *radical obedience* has been the most rewarding and fulfilling experience. This quiet space in Ellendale, North Dakota, is changing the world. Men and women are leaving Trinity and impacting and transforming this nation and nations around the world, with the amazing love of Jesus. The best is still ahead of us.

As I sit quietly, pondering and reflecting over our 13 years of service at Trinity my heart is strangely warmed. I did not want to come to this seemingly desolate place. However, the past 13 years have been the most rewarding of our entire ministry.

As the sun rises, heralding a new day, my spirit is alive and ready for the day. The amber hues filter through the blinds of our old Prairie Victorian home, filling me with hope for the season ahead. In this quiet space of Ellendale, North Dakota, men and women are preparing to serve their God and see families transformed, marriages mended, broken lives made whole; at the same time dysfunctional people are functioning again, and young people and children are being redeemed and restored. Trinity Bible College and Graduate School is a unique and wonderful place that is in the business of preparing men and women for ministry.

I have sometimes asked God why He would place a Bible College and Graduate School in a seemingly insignificant place. God showed me that most often, our influence grows in the midst of walking a path of *radical obedience* and insignificance. It is in the quiet place, the wilderness, and the monastic spaces, that we gain internal strength.

Trinity is a space where we place huge emphasis on servanthood. It is our earnest prayer that students who leave this beautiful place called Trinity, will be clothed in humility, have hearts filled with passion, and have hands ready to serve wherever God leads them. Our desire during the remainder of the years left to us, is that we will see thousands of young people released into ministry to build the Kingdom of God in whatever sphere God calls them.

Prayerful Pause:

Radical obedience is never reckless but it does require us putting our trust in the Lord. Sometimes our plans and dreams are not God's purposes for our lives. We have learned that God knows best. God knows our hearts and He knows what we need better than we do. You may find yourself in a transition, like we did thirteen years ago. This is where trust comes into the situation. As Hebrews says, we need to keep our focus on Jesus, not on the circumstances surrounding us but on His promises and consequently keep pressing on. Sometimes in trying situations we tend to focus on the problem and in so doing we are incapable of focusing on God's promises. As difficult as it is, pause now to ask God to help you to refocus. Keep your eye on the goal and do not be discouraged by negative thoughts or situations.

The book of Numbers, chapter 13, is a challenging story. The leaders of Israel were sent out by Moses to explore the land that God had promised to give them. They went and explored the land as Moses asked them to. However, their perceptions were distorted by their negativity. Instead of seeing potential, they only saw pitfalls. Negativity distorted their view, and it had dire consequences for all the people of Israel. We encourage you to keep your focus on Jesus and ensure that you do not cloud your view with negative thoughts. Negativity can be like a cancer and eat away at your courage and your joy. Pray that God will see you through this season. Remember the Psalmist said that weeping endures for the night, and then the morning brings joy. We have found that the darker the night the greater the joy when the morning does come. May your morning be filled with joy, gladness, and radiance.

For those of you who are contemplating full time ministry, may we encourage you to pursue your dream. Prepare yourself for the task ahead and be willing to go and do whatever God has for you. We can assure you that God will order your steps and meet your needs as He has always done for us. Do not delay His call on your life. Let your response be quick and ready and then ensure that you do everything to ready yourself for service.

An Open Letter

Lord stamp eternity on my eyeballs

JONATHAN EDWARDS

CAROL

Dear Student,

We live in a world that is in constant flux, and navigating the ever-changing cultural milieu can be daunting. I want to emphasize three virtues that I think will help you as you seek to serve God. There are many more virtues but I think these particular ones will help you to focus and stay the journey to the end.

Firstly, I want to emphasize the virtue of humility. In my years of ministry, I have seen too many men and women who started their ministry with humility but as their influence grew so too did their pride. Never think that you are too great to stoop down and touch the leper. When that happens, dear student, you have arrived at the point of being far too big in your own eyes. I am persuaded that Jesus does not view success as we often do. Success is simply being like Jesus. Success will be to hear those words: "Well done, good and faithful servant." That will look different for everyone. You see whether you are preaching to thousands or preparing food for others or worshipping on a platform, or sweeping the sanctuary; what matters is that you are doing everything with all your heart and with the right attitude. Jesus modelled humility for us and to stay in ministry for the long haul, I urge you to walk in humility.

Secondly, I want to exhort you to compassion or put another way, love. This is a virtue that will keep you serving, even when you are exhausted, discouraged or disappointed. Compassion is the one virtue that will hold you to the task. You have to love people in spite of all their flaws and serve them, even when they fail you. This is because you love them and having compassion will help to ground you. There have been times when I have felt discouraged beyond what any words could describe; what has kept me going, is seeing the faces of the needy and knowing that there is nothing else I would rather do than serve them, encourage them, and see them succeed.

Thirdly, I appeal to you to live with integrity. Nothing will ever replace character. I often tell our students at Trinity that charisma is a wonderful characteristic but it will not sustain you in ministry. What will keep you the long haul, is integrity. Live your life with integrity and authenticity. Doing the right thing is not always easy and it can be costly. Integrity will keep you from mishandling finances. It will keep you faithful to your spouse. It will enable you to make the right decision, even when a more lucrative or influential position is more appealing. Integrity will guard you from hubris and ensure that you will never think more highly of yourself than you should. Integrity is doing the right thing even when no one else is watching. Integrity is the one virtue that will help you to stay the course. Humility, love, and integrity, are three ingredients that are essential for service in God's kingdom. Of course, we could expand on patience, self-control, kindness and gentleness. All of the virtues are important but I major on three that I think will help to keep you focused on the task before you.

Your whole life is ahead of you. Amazing opportunities will present themselves. Make each day count and seize every moment. You are deeply loved and valued by your heavenly Father. Make your life count and consequently make a difference in God's world which bears fruit for eternity.

Dear Parent,

What an incredible privilege we have as parents—to bring children into the world and help to shape and form them for their future. And yet, also what a challenging time in history to be tasked with this responsibility. As a parent and grandparent, allow me to bare my heart before you. If I were to give three pieces of advice; this is what they would be:

Firstly, always put God first. I have heard parents complaining that their children are not serving God; yet, those same parents never made God a priority in their home. Sports was always prioritized over church, school could never be missed because learning was so important yet if that same child was tired or not feeling the best it was fine to miss church. If the child was exhausted from a heavy load at school it was considered legitimate that they could catch up on sleep on Sunday and miss spiritual nourishment and challenge so they could be ready for school on Monday. What sort of message is that giving a child? As a parent you might be thinking that church is not necessarily prioritizing God, but it is a signal to your family that it is important to have community and that you are going to make church a priority because God is your priority. Remember, if God is first, then you also have to trust your children to His care.

Secondly, the best gift you will ever give your children is the security of knowing your marriage is solid and wholesome. This is not a letter of condemnation to those who have failed relationships because I understand that there are broken homes and at times, irreconcilable differences. However, that does not take away from this important issue. Living in a world that cares little about faithfulness and marriage, can we model a different way to our children? If you are separated from your spouse at least honor them in front of your children. Do your level best to keep peace and harmony in the relationship and never undermine each other. Your children need the security of a safe and godly environment. The way you accomplish this is by ensuring God is always first and every decision is made with that emphasis foremost in the family's minds.

Thirdly, make lasting memories with your children. We love our children and want the best for their lives. You can give your children material things, money, expensive vacations but all of that will be forgotten one day. Your children will forget the expensive TV you bought. They will never remember the money you spent on technology or other items. What your children and young people will never forget is the memories you made with them. The picnics you enjoyed together, that cost nothing but a few sandwiches and drinks. The walks in the forest where you listened to their hearts. Those moments when you held your little girl in your arms because her heart was broken over some silly boy are so important. You didn't undermine her pain you held her and cried with her. Again, your continual presence at their important events and your loud cheering at every big and small achievement they accomplished are the moments they will never forget. Events like holding your daughter's hand in the car on her wedding day, when not a word is spoken but as parents, you know that your love for this precious, God given gift, will never diminish with the passing of time. The pride that fills your heart when your boy tells you that he has found the girl that he was looking for and you know that His love for God will sustain that relationship is what counts. Yes, make beautiful happy memories that will fill your children's hearts long after you have gone because you laid a good foundation for their whole life to build upon with God at the center.

May we build lasting marriages, secure homes, and ensure that God is central in every part of our family's lives. This my friend is what I call success.

PAUL

Reflecting on fifty years of Christian ministry there are things that are much less important now than in previous years. The joy of being less confrontational and hopefully more gracious with those that do not agree with you is a treasure of mature age. This is a wonderful season of life. Tolerance without compromise, the wisdom of much experience, and the desire to end well, all combine to make each day a happy and fulfilling one.

On the other hand, some deep convictions become more focused with age and experience. There are deep desires that long to save younger people from pain and distress and equally to endeavor to ensure that values and principles that have worked well across the decades are preserved. And so, with a humble heart but with passionate candor I write this open letter.

To Christian Leaders

My fellow leaders your responsibility is immense, and the next generation looks closely at you. Arrogance, posturing and bluff are demeaning and way below who you are and why God called you in the first place. Authenticity, care and humility will always make you shine and have the impact that you pray you would have. In kindness I ask you:

- Always be gentle with young people. They need your guidance and advice, but a harsh word wrongly spoken can take years to heal.
- Decide to lead with enthusiasm. There is enough going on in most people's lives not to be burdened with a sarcastic, lethargic, and uninvolved leader. Better to find something else to do with your life than impose a mood on others.
- Keep the long game in view. Simply put, the disappointments of today can be the building blocks of joyful opportunity in the future. No disappointment, no cruel action, and no scheme of a wicked person, should dampen your resolve to get up each day, serve God with gladness and then finish strong.

To Christian Educators

My fellow educator this job is a difficult one. It is made more difficult in many of our contexts because we lack a basic theology of education and possibly even of work itself. Our church context is dominated (rightly so) by pastors who have the daily burden of the flock. Then, importantly, we compete in a world of secular universities and colleges that really are only concerned for content and not character. Add to this the unenviable task of creating the narrative that the added cost of a private, Christian education is worth it, and we have created the scenario where the average tenure of a President in a Christian university or college is less than six years. Creating plausibility is a challenge. Thus:

- For theological educators, do not tire in this vital task. Draw deep from the well of biblical and human wisdom that everything in our lives is much better if done in community. This includes the connected learning community of a college, a cohort or an intentional web-based community. Please, my friends, be advocates for communities that learn together, grow together and serve together.

- For those who have the privilege of leading Christian liberal art institutions, stay strong. Yours is the task to persuade our constituencies of the value of an education in an institution that is fundamentally Christian. Your faculty must believe and practice the Bible. Huge resources must be allocated to ensuring that your students live out their faith experiences. I pray with you that as parents entrust their students to your care not one will be lost, not a single household disappointed, and that your institution will be the source of a river of well trained and educated, Christ-following men and women entering the workforce.

- For those facilitating short-term training opportunities or ministerial preparation schools, fight with all your strength to avoid the potential of lowering the standards of academic rigor. Never compare and contrast in order to gain a cheap advantage over residential or degree granting institutions. This is unbecoming and will spawn people who celebrate ignorance without even knowing it.

Christian leaders, Christian educators, may we pass to the next generation more than we received from our fathers. May we give to them an example of grace and humility. May we inspire them to excellence and achievement. May God be honored and the nations blessed.